Our Ancestors From the Stars

June Rye

London | New York

Published by Clink Street Publishing 2018

Copyright © 2018

First edition.

The author asserts the moral right under the Copyright, Designs and Patents Act 1988 to be identified as the author of this work.

All rights reserved. No part of this publication may be reproduced, stored in a retrieval system or transmitted, in any form or by any means without the prior consent of the author, nor be otherwise circulated in any form of binding or cover other than that with which it is published and without a similar condition being imposed on the subsequent purchaser.

ISBN:
978-1-912562-24-4

Contents

About the Author	3
Acknowledgements	5
Introduction	7
Myths and Legends	**11**
Myths	11
Legends	11
Light At The End Of The Tunnel	**13**
'One Fact and Several Observations	13
A Brief History of the Human Race on Planet Earth	**17**
Body, Mind and Spirit	17
The Body	17
What Happens to The Soul After You Die?	18
The Missing Link	19
Human DNA	21
The Creation of Adam	23
Other 'Adams'	24
Star Children	25
Indigo Children	26
Crystal Children	26
Rainbow Children	27
The Universe, Planets and Stars	**29**
The Universe	29
The Solar System	29
The Earth and Moon	30
Fast Facts	30
The History of The Constellations	30
Wormholes and Portals	31

The Seeding of the Stars; The Birth of the Alien Species	33
Note	33
In the Beginning	34
Various 'Edens'	42
The Anunnaki	45
Atlantis	49
Lemuria (Mu)	51
The Anunnaki in Africa and the Pleiades	55
The Great Flood	59
The Great Deluge	59
After the Deluge	60
The Anunnaki after the Deluge	62
Nuclear War	64
The Gene Map of the Nations	66
Identity of the Gods	67
Unravelling the Gods	67
The Identity of the Serpent Gods	69
The Names of the Gods	71
The present World History Timeline found in our History Books	73
The History of the Caduceus	74
The Reason the Ancient Gods Are Depicted with Animal Heads	75
Giants	77
Ancient Underground Tunnels And Cities	83
Subterranean Tunnels and Underground Alien Bases	86
Secrets of the Subterranean Cities	87
Underwater Bases	87
Svalbard Global Seed Vault in Norway	88
Crop Circles and Stone Circles	91
Crop Circles	91
Stone Circles	94
Stonehenge in England	96
Southern Africa	97
Great Zimbabwe	100
To Sum Up	101
Megaliths	103
Mount Shoria in Southern Siberia	103
Yonaguni Island in Japan	104
Easter Island	105
Kailasa Temple in Western India	106
Gobekli Tepe in Turkey	108
Angkor Wat in Cambodia	108

Ta Prohm in Cambodia	110
Further Examples of Megalithic Structures	111
Pyramids and Earth's Energy Grid	**113**
Why Were the Pyramids Built?	118
The Alien Species Involved in Planet Earth's Evolution	**121**
Alien Abductions	**125**
Elizabeth Klarer	126
Disclosure	**129**
Disinformation	129
Press Conference Overview	130
Don Phillips	130
Colonel Philip Corso	130
Major-General Wilfred de Brouwer	131
Timothy Good	133
Larry Holcombe	133
Paul Hellyer	134
Dr Michael E. Salla, MA, PhD	134
UFO Sightings by NASA Astronauts	135
Illuminati	136
To Sum Up	137
Final Thoughts	**141**
Suggested Sites to Visit	143
Popular Videos	143

About the Author

June Rye was born in South Africa and emigrated to England in 1978. Her Book *Be Healthy and Fit the Wholefood way* was published in South Africa in 1977, and her eBook *The Dawn of the Age of Aquarius* in the UK in 2012. Her husband Charles sadly passed away in 2013. She has two children and two grandchildren.

Acknowledgements

I wish to thank my editor Kimberley Humphries for the marvellous job she did in shaping my haphazard chapters into a coherent, readable book.

Website: http://www.morethan-words.com

Contact: kimberley@morethan-words.com / 07754 778910

I also like to acknowledge the cover design, created by talented graphic designer, Alice Kennedy.

Website: http://alicekennedy.wixsite.com/aykdesign

Contact Page: http://alicekennedy.wixsite.com/aykdesign/contact

Introduction

Writing a sequel to *Aquarius* never entered my mind. In fact, just the thought of getting involved with anything to do with visions and other dimensions made me feel quite ill. The past thirty-two years have been grey years. They started in May 1985, and were followed by years of stress and trauma from receiving periodic flashes of visions which for years made no sense. Then, around 2008, my husband Charles was diagnosed with the early onset of dementia and his health gradually deteriorated, until by 2011 he had become completely bed-ridden. (I did, however, manage to get *Aquarius* published in January 2012.) The years when my husband was ill were very difficult, but I was very fortunate to have carers who came in twice daily to help with his needs. His last two years were quite surreal. He had been such a vibrant, strong personality and in the end he became a quiet, gentle soul so appreciative of everything that was being done for him. He died peacefully at the end of November 2013. (Three weeks prior to his death, my mum passed away in South Africa at the beginning of that same month, November 2013. She had been suffering from Alzheimer's.)

The emotion that followed wasn't a feeling of sadness, because I was relieved their suffering had come to an end and that they were both at peace; it was more a feeling of complete inner exhaustion. I felt it was time to go 'home', too, and that my mission in this life had been fulfilled. I hung around feeling tired and despondent, and I waited and waited . . . and nothing happened. I mentioned this to an astrologer who, at the time, was doing a karmic astrology chart for each of my grandchildren, and she said to me, "Rest assured, if you're still alive there is obviously more you still have to do . . ." I realised then that it was time to wake up and start living again.

I remembered that I had made a note of the four past lives – which I mentioned in *Aquarius*, but declined to include all the details – and decided to write an autobiography especially for my grandchildren (not for publication, I hasten to add!) about growing up on a South African farm during the 1940s. This was completed just before my seventy-ninth birthday, in June 2016, and I was feeling rather pleased with myself.

But, a few weeks later, I woke up in shock with the most frightening visions of planets, spaceships, stars and weird grey beings whizzing around in my head. And the first thing I said out loud was, "Oh please, God, not the visions again!" and burst out crying. Then it all stopped and I became aware of a loving being's presence beside me, and I recognised him to be the elder who had guided me through the various dimensions I wrote about in *Aquarius*. He then told me which star cluster our soul group came from, and that we hadn't been home for the past 2,000 years because our work had been here on Earth, specifically to spread, teach and establish Christian communities throughout the world during the Age of Pisces. But, he explained, as we were now moving into this new age – the Age of Aquarius – there were more mature members of the human race now grown up enough to cope with the new information which is already starting to filter out into the media and the world in general. He told me I was to write about UFOs, alien abductions, and visitors from outer space and the reason why this information has been kept under wraps all these years, and how they have guided and manipulated the human race for thousands of years. This frightened me very much, as I didn't think it was my place to mention this. But he assured me that prominent psychiatrists and high-up government officials have already spoken out on this subject, and all I had to do was to compile this information, and write it as I would a thesis and have it published as an e-book.

As I started trawling through the internet, I gradually started to understand the reason why I became involved in a search for spirituality in 1985 by finding that those who had written about their experiences, and the subjects I was instructed to write about. It all began around that same time, as if all the 'messengers' had been programmed to start their individual research or initiation from around the 1980s, timed to move gently into the new millennium – and this is obviously still going on because of all the latest technology, new discoveries and inventions that are happening faster and faster.

It is interesting to note here that the Mayan calendar predicted that the end of the world (thought to be true by many!) was to happen on the 21st December 2012; but this actually indicated that we were at the end of the old teachings and the beginning of a new era of knowledge and discovery. And that after spending time learning and trying to absorb the new scientific information regarding our own creation, new archaeological discoveries, the discovery of lost civilizations (thought to be mythical) which existed ten to fifteen thousand years ago, not to mention the fact that our DNA contains strands of extraterrestrial DNA, it had become quite obvious that over time all the old textbooks would eventually have to be rewritten.

So it has been my instruction to collate and document this new information here in one concise book. (There are many other sources of information, and these are included at the end of the book under 'Suggested Sites to Visit'.) It is my hope that it will enlighten you as it has done me.

Myths and Legends

Myths

A myth is a story based on tradition or legend, and which has a deep symbolic meaning. A myth conveys a 'truth' to those who tell it and hear it, rather than necessarily recording a true event. Although some myths can be accounts of actual events, they have become transformed by symbolic meanings or shifted in time or place. Myths are often used to explain universal and local beginnings, and involve supernatural beings. The great power of the meaning of these stories to the culture in which they developed is a major reason why they have survived as long as they have – in some cases for thousands of years.

Legends

A legend is a semi-true story which has been passed on from person to person and has important meaning or symbolism for the culture in which it originates. A legend usually includes an element of truth, or is based on historic facts, but with mystical qualities. Legends usually involve heroic characters or fantastic places and often encompass the spiritual beliefs of the cultures in which they originate.

In the light of all the latest research, it would now seem that the myths and legends of the past were about events which actually happened, and these are what we will discuss here.

(Source: Myths and Legends: Teachers)

June Rye

Light At The End Of The Tunnel

As this book is about UFOs and extraterrestrials, I feel it's only fitting to start the ball rolling by quoting from a book by Paul Hellyer entitled *Light at The End of The Tunnel* (2010).

The Honourable Paul Hellyer is a former Canadian minister of defence, who presided over the country's armed forces during the time of the Cold War. In 2005 he made headlines by publicly announcing the existence of alien beings visiting and living on our planet. He is the first high-ranking official to openly admit to this fact, and he has kindly given me permission to share the information below:

'One Fact and Several Observations

One fact is beyond intelligent dispute. UFOs, or space ships, originating from planets other from our own, are as real as the airplanes flying overhead! They have been visiting Earth for decades and, in all probability, for centuries or millennia. The following are some observations based on evidence and literature believed to be substantially reliable.

(a) The size of the vehicles range from the very small Foo Foos (balls of light which follow and hover around planes), that were

probably unmanned but intelligently controlled reconnaissance machines, to very large "mother ships" wider than a mile across. The mother ships may carry smaller craft capable of operating independently, at least for short periods. The most frequently observed space ships have been estimated to be in the order of twenty-five feet to one hundred and fifty feet in diameter.

(b) The visitors comprise more than one species from more than one source. These include Zeta Reticuli, the Pleiades, Orion, Andromeda and Altair star systems. The Short Greys, as they are called, have been the most often reported, and they are the ones recovered from various crashes, including Roswell. There are others including Tall Greys, Nordic Blonds, Semitics and Reptilians, each with their own distinct characteristics.

(c) They appear to be benign because they certainly possessed the technology to immobilize our power sources, and command and control facilities. General Nathan Twining an Air Force Regulation 200-2 issued when he was Chief of Staff in 1954, wrote under the heading Air Defence: "To date the flying objects reported have imposed no threat to the security of the United States and its possessions." Despite the assurance, untold sums have been spent developing the aliens' own technology in an effort to control them militarily.

(d) The visitors' technology is much more advanced than our own. For example, they have craft that can travel faster than the speed of light that we have long assumed to be impossible. Earthlings have reverse-engineered some of their technology retrieved from crash sites that may include advanced lasers, integrated circuitry, fibre optics networks, accelerated particle-beam devices, and even the Kevlar materials in bulletproof vests. It is widely believed that the United States has developed anti-gravity space vehicles that are indistinguishable from those of the star visitors but which may not yet have the same highly developed propulsion systems.

(e) Some of the visiting space ships have demonstrated their ability to beam both humans and cattle from earth to their ships in a shaft of bluish-grey light. Some species, including the greys, have the capacity to walk through doors and walls that we know and describe as solid objects.

(f) It is difficult to determine the agendas of the different species. Some, the greys specifically, extract human sperm and ova for the purpose of replenishing their own reproductive capability after allegedly genetically engineering themselves to the point where live births are difficult or impossible. This is the principle purpose of the mass abductions. What is not clear is whether they have been given permission to do this in exchange for technology, or whether it is done without permission because they have the technological ability to do it on their own initiative.

(g) The question of cattle mutilations is also a grey area. One school of thought suggests that the incredibly precise incisions, far superior to what our medical profession use in current practice, is related solely to the harvesting of genetic material. Another school argues that the cattle mutilations are primarily a wide-scale experiment to determine the amount of residual radioactive contamination that exists as a result of the earlier testing and use of nuclear weapons.

(h) There is a spiritual overtone to much of the extraterrestrial activity. Reports from many sources indicate that at least some species of star visitors are much more spiritual than Earthlings, and more reverential towards the Creator, the Source, the One, Allah, the Great Spirit – God by whatever name He is known.

The late Dr John Mack, an American secular Jewish psychiatrist who became a world leader in interviewing abductees – or "experiencers" as he preferred to call them – came to this conclusion in his startling book Passport to the Cosmos: *"Although the aliens are not themselves gods – their behaviour is sometimes anything but godlike – the abductees consistently report that the beings seem closer to the Godhead than we are, acting as messengers, guardian spirits, or angels, intermediaries between us and the Divine Source."*

(Source Paul Hellyer, Light at The End of The Tunnel, *2010 http://www.exopaedia.org/Hellyer%2C+Paul See also: 'Disclosure')*

But before we can start investigating UFOs and aliens, we need to understand how we fit into all of this.

A Brief History of the Human Race on Planet Earth

Body, Mind and Spirit

Man (and woman) kind are made up of three parts: body, mind and spirit.

The Body
This is your physical part which consists mainly of water, flesh and bone. It is the thing we can see.

The Mind
The mind contains your psyche (your soul). Your mind is the place where your thoughts come from. It is not your brain, but whatever it is that generates your thoughts and emotions. The brain is the place that houses the blueprint of your existence right from the beginning of your own creation. There are 240 miles of neuronal threads in the human brain – enough to stretch from Earth to the moon. On every micro-metre of these threads there are 240,000 units of information encoded in your brain.

The Spirit
This is the energy, the electricity which drives the workings of your mind and body. This energy comes from the cosmos. Call it what you wish: the breath of God, solar energy, or a sprinkling of stardust from another star system.

Withdraw the energy, your physical body stops working and you die.

What Happens to The Soul After You Die?

Your soul lives on in another dimension for a rest and further study in preparation for your next life on the earth plane. The younger souls rest in peace for a while before they set off again, oblivious as to what their next life plan entails. The more evolved souls are involved in planning the blueprint for their next life. This is carefully planned by choosing the correct environment, the country, the sort of parents which are needed for particular lessons to learn for further spiritual growth, as well as for karma issues that need to be faced, also, to set the milestones for when or where you are to meet a certain person, or to be at a certain place, or to face a certain situation. To the human mind this seems to be an impossible task, but with the technology available to the guardians of our planet it is a mere touch of a button on the universal computer to slot your life plan into the overall plan for planet Earth, without disturbing the path of any of the trillions of other beings within this system.

It took man over a million years to progress from using stones as he found them to the realization that they can be chipped and flaked to better purpose.

It took another 500,000 years before Neanderthal man mastered the concept of stone tools, and a further 50,000 years before crops were cultivated and metallurgy was discovered.

Hence, by all scales of evolutionary reckoning, we should still be far removed from any basic understanding of mathematics, engineering or science. But here we are, only 7,000 years later, landing a probe on Mars.

This raises three questions:

- Where did this knowledge come from?
- How did this knowledge appear to develop mostly within the same timeframe in the various civilised nations on the planet?
- Where did the various races on the planet come from?

The Missing Link

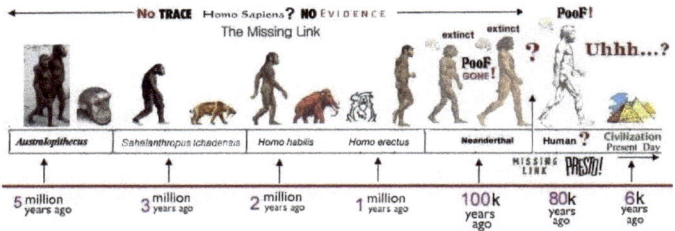

Missing link Homo Sapien timeline

In 1974 it was thought that 'the missing link' had been found when the bone fossils of a female belonging to the hominid species Australopithecus Afarensis was found in the Awash Valley in Ethiopia. She was named 'Lucy' from the song *Lucy in the Sky with Diamonds* by the Beatles, which was played loudly and repeatedly in the expedition camp all evening after the excavation team's first day. The Lucy specimen is dated to about 3.2 million years ago, and until 1997 it was scientifically assumed that *all* of the human species on planet earth had evolved from her.

It was through genetic testing done in 1997 that proof was finally achieved that modern humans (Homo sapiens sapiens) had not the slightest trace of ancestry from even the Cro-Magnons. Similar testing found that Homo erectus dated back to only 40,000 years ago in Java, rather than having died out 200,000 years ago as originally thought.

None of these forerunners evolved from each other either. They all seem to possess singular characteristics unrelated to the others, meaning that their genetics evolved separately from each other. Then, too, some mysteriously died out while others survived.

It is thought the cause of this was that an experiment went wrong by mixing too many of the blood groups together. This 'tinkering' with our genes is also the cause of all the degenerative disorders such as Alzheimer's disease, amyotrophic lateral sclerosis and Huntington's disease, to name just a few.

The black, brown, red, yellow and the white races are all descended from colonization occurring from various extraterrestrial species that settled here on Earth, and/or occasionally visited the planet. Some of these species have been colonising this planet for a few million years, and it is only now, at the beginning of this new age, when the human race has sufficiently mentally and spiritually evolved, that they are making us aware of their presence.

Logically it is easy to understand that as we were seeded by the various star nations, we have inherited their genetic and ethnic diversity. This also covers the diversity of our physical appearance, such as red hair and freckles, blond hair and blue eyes, black hair and brown eyes, and so on. Not to mention the differences in our blood types, such as RH negative, RH positive, A, B, AB and O blood types.

I should mention also that the hundreds of species occupying the universe have been engaged in galactic battles fought over millions of years in and around all the galaxies and planets in the universe. For example, the stories of the battles fought between Lucifer and his dark fallen angels against the good guys are told in mythical form, and the Science Fiction films appearing on our screens reflect what has been going on for millions of years, well before the dinosaurs lived on our planet.

Human DNA

DNA is a unit of heredity which is transferred from a parent to offspring and is held to determine some characteristic of the offspring.

The following are short summaries from *Blood Prints of the Gods* by Brian Foster, *Species with Amnesia* by Robert Sepehr, *Humanity's Extra-terrestrial Origin* by Dr Arthur David Horn, and Craig Venter of *The Human Genome Project*:

Our DNA is encoded with messages from other civilizations. Aliens programmed the DNA molecules so that when we reached a certain level of intelligence, we would be able to access their information and they could therefore 'teach' us about ourselves and how to progress. Human DNA variation now turns out to be over seven times greater than the ninety-nine percent that was thought before. In the Human Genome Project, studies show a two to three percent difference in the genetic structure between race groupDNA was discovered fifty years ago, and as scientists began to unravel and decode the human DNA molecule they found something amazingly unexpected: a computer 'language' composed of some three billion genetic DNA that actually store information – the detailed instruction for assembling proteins – in the form of a four-character digital code.

The quantum of the information in our human DNA is comparably equal to twelve sets of the Encyclopædia Britannica, an amazing 384 volumes-worth of detailed data that would fill forty-eight feet of required library shelves.

The coding regions of DNA have exactly the same relevant properties as a computer of language. Just whose mind, or what entity, could shrink and miniaturize such information and place our DNA's enormous number of 'letters' in their correct sequence as a genetic building block instruction manual, and orchestrate the DNA information storage system of the entire universe? Determine that the pattern of base pairs in a DNA molecule specifies the gene?

But the DNA molecule is the medium, it's not the message. It is, in a way, the hard drive storage for all the lifetimes of our ancestors who have added their genes in order to create ours. It is also the container for various elements of cosmic knowledge and, especially, for the secrets regarding the cosmic connection of man to his creator.

After the devastation caused by the deluge, our ET creators set about seeding the planet all over again. Forests were planted and civilizations were created using the DNA preserved by the various creator ETs before the flood. People were placed in various parts of the world and taught to cultivate food, and learn animal husbandry, weaving and pottery etc. The elders were taught to read and write, and pyramids were built in specific places especially aligned with particular star clusters in order to find their way to and from home in the heavens. The creators set themselves up as gods, some more so than others. All in all, it took about another 7,000 years to restore order after the flood.

The DNA specifically preserved by the Anunnaki creator god Enki was their own human/Orion/Sirian/Pleiadian/reptilian DNA. (Interestingly, this seems to be the DNA thread found in many prominent world leaders.)

A brief analysis of the Anunnaki DNA is as follows:

Our behaviour and appearance basically depends on what proportion of DNA genes we have inherited from the above set of genes. The Orion brings out the feminine part; the Sirians are physically short, stocky, hairy and mostly male-orientated; the reptilians are aggressive/domineering, and the Pleiadian are even-tempered, and tall with blue eyes and a fair completion. It would also seem that our RH Negative blood group was inherited from reptilian DNA.

There are three parts to the brain, the reptilian brain being the oldest of the three, and it is worth noting that the term *'reptilian'* refers to our primitive, instinctive brain function that is shared by all reptiles and mammals, including humans. It is the most powerful and oldest of our coping brain functions, since without it we would not be alive.

(Source: http://www.copingskills4kids.net/Reptilian_Coping_Brain.html)

The Creation of Adam

Genesis 2-21.22 (KJV) reads: *'And the Lord God caused a deep sleep to fall on Adam, and as he slept He took one of his ribs, and closed up the flesh in its place. Then the rib which the Lord God had taken from man He made into a woman, and He brought her to the man.'*

The following story of Adam's creation comes from the Sumerian clay tablet, the Atra-Hasis Text, dating from about 432,000 years ago. It states that the sperm of a young Anunnaki male was mixed with an apewoman's egg in a laboratory flask and put into the womb of a female Anunnaki. The hybrids could not procreate; therefore, female Anunnaki had to act each time as birth-goddesses. These hybrids were perfected over many thousands of years through trial and error until the perfect model was achieved. They named him *Adam*.

Some seals show a goddess, flanked by the Tree of Life and laboratory flasks, holding up a new-born being.

The being that was thus produced, which is repeatedly referred to in Mesopotamian texts as a 'model man' or a 'mold', was apparently the right creature, for the gods then clamoured for duplicates.

(Source: https://www.bibliotecapleyades.net/sitchin/ planeta12/12planeteng_12.htm)

Other 'Adams'

There were many other prototypes of 'Adams' created by various alien species in different regions of the planet. But basically, there were five sub-species who differed in pigmentation and characteristics depending on which alien species had created them and the natural environment in which they lived.

In the Gobi Desert, they appeared as yellow; in Carpathian region (the southern part of Europe and Russian, Persia and Caucasian mountains) as white; in the Atlantean and American locality as red; from the remnants of ancient Mu (Lemuria), the people from the Philippines, Polynesia and Bali as brown; and in Africa and Sudanese territory as black.

Because of this manipulation of human genes, it took thousands of years to create an Adam and a mate for him. Many DNA 'recipes' were tried and subsequently destroyed, until the Adam in each race was deemed to be acceptable by the original founders of creation.

The influence of the Anunnaki, as well as all the other ET species that created us, has influenced every aspect of human life. Many of us have inherited through their genes their patriarchal culture of violence and vengeance: an eye for an eye from the reptilian species, for example, and this in our engineered DNA.

According to Lyssa Royal, author and channeller, and *Galactic Information,* the Adam prototype for the Asian races, who are basically the Japanese, Chinese, Mongolian,

Vietnamese, Malays, New Guineans as well as the Tibetans, Koreans and Siberians, were made up of DNA from the Zeta Reticuli Greys, and these beings are the ones who are small with large dark eyes – the Paleiadians and Sirians. (The
DNA of the latter two species were already in the other prototypes.)

(Source: https://www.bibliotecapleyades.net/vida_alien/alien_lyssaroyal01.htm)

In the year 2000, the University of Pavia, Italy, did a genetic study of European men. They found that eighty percent of them had a direct lineage to Central Asia, and the other twenty percent to the Middle East. This supports the statement that the Sumerians entered Central Asia and then migrated into Europe and the Middle East. This also nullifies the theory of Africa as the birthplace of mankind. There is absolutely no genetic connection from Europe to Africa.

Star Children

There have been many titles given to the new generation of children: 'star children, 'gifted children', "millennium children', 'star seeds' or 'special children'. However, from the spiritual perspective, they are referred to as the 'indigo, crystal and rainbow children'. These names are related to the colour in their auras and the energy patterns. They have arrived in the last three decades and are still arriving on our planet.

These children are very creative and some have heightened psychic abilities of clear seeing (clairvoyance), clear hearing (clairaudience), clear feeling (clairsentience), and clear knowing (claircognizance). These abilities allow them to hear or see spirits or angels, and detect dishonesty, or have accurate inner knowing about events, situations or people when they first encounter them. They are sensitive and intuitive.

They've come with a special mission to assist Earth and humanity with our transition and rebirth to a higher consciousness. They are here to help us with ascension, and an accelerated soul evolution for its inhabitants at this special time on Earth.

Indigo Children

The main influx was between 1970-1990; although many scout indigos arrived before 1970, and some indigos are still arriving with characteristics of the crystal children, or a cross-over between indigos and crystals.

They have indigo auras which are connected with the third eye's frequency. These children are intelligent, quick learners and technologically orientated; some have amazing memories. They are very academic in situations where they are able to stay focused, and are content in their environment and people they are with. They are direct, determined and confident. Many display a warrior temperament, and yet are easily frustrated with routines, rituals, rules and regulations.

Some other negative characteristics of Indigos are that they are hyperactive, impatient, inconsiderate and disrespectful. This relates to their high level of creative energies. It is therefore important to help Indigo children to divert their energies to creative pursuits such as music, creative writing, arts and craft, and even sport, to keep them in focus.

They are wise old souls and natural leaders who are returning to lead us into a new age of cooperation, creativity and functional society where there will be no corruption and deceit.

Crystal Children

The main influx was around the year 2000, although crystal scouts came much earlier. These are very powerful children.

Crystal children's main purpose is to take us to the next level in our evolution. They awake our inner power and divinity with their innate love, wisdom and peace. They create a safe and a more secure world.

According to Doreen Virtue, crystal children have opalescent auras, with beautiful multi-colours in pastel hues. They have innate spiritual gifts. Many have telepathic and psychic abilities. They are very intuitive and extremely sensitive to energies and emotions. It is very common for crystal children to start speaking at a later age of three or four, and some to have speech difficulties because of their telepathy. For this reason, some have been diagnosed with autism by medical practitioners.

Similar to indigo, crystal children are very creative and resourceful. They too have high energies, yet they remain calm and peaceful.

Rainbow Children

According to Doreen Virtue, the rainbow children have recently appeared, in the last five years, and are still arriving on our planet. They are fearless and pure givers. They radiate rainbow energy: a very high vibrational energy of unconditional love.

The rainbow children have never lived on this planet before, and they're going straight to the crystal children as their mums and dads. These children are entirely fearless of everybody. They're little avatars who are all about service. These are children who are only here to give. Rainbow children are already at their spiritual peek.

Unlike indigo children, most crystal children have not been incarnated on Earth before; and certainly the rainbow children have never lived on Earth before. They have evolved from other planets/systems where they have resolved all their karma and personal learning lessons. Thus, their focus is purely on service and humanity.

Similar to crystal children, rainbow children are likely to be diagnosed with autism by medical practitioners because they are in their own world. They have difficulties in relating to human emotions, especially the negative and dysfunctional ones. Like little Buddha and Jesus, they give and love unconditionally, and are uncorrupted by negative emotional judgements.

Rainbow children are fearless and pure givers because they are already fully evolved. They have fully merged with their higher self and with the source, the Creator. Fears and the lower self are no longer part of them. As one evolves and ascends, the essence of 'oneness' and selfless service becomes their only soul mission.

(Source: www.thepyramidoflight.com Click on http://thepyramidoflight.com/articles/children-of-the-stars/

See also: Mary Rodwell – "Who is The New Human?" (EXCLUSIVE on-location in Los Angeles) https://www.youtube.com/watch?v=cUcqfz6-Rzc)

The Universe, Planets and Stars

The Universe

Scientists estimate that there must be about 10,000 billion billion stars in the universe – more than the number of grains of sand on all the beaches on Earth.

Our galaxy is called the Milky Way and is one of the largest galaxies in a cluster of about forty-five galaxies. Most of these have no particular shape, and are much smaller than the Milky Way.

The Solar System

Earth is just one of the many objects that orbit the star we call the Sun. Our sun's family consists of eight planets, five dwarf planets, hundreds of moons, millions of comets and asteroids, and a myriad of other gasses and dust. All these things together are called the Solar System. The four small planets closest to our sun – Mercury, Venus, Earth and Mars – are made of rock; while the four outer planets are much larger and made mostly of gases. The Solar System is big: the Voyager space craft took twelve years to reach Neptune, the outermost planet.

The Earth and Moon

Earth's nearest neighbour is the moon, our planet's only natural satellite. The moon is about one quarter the diameter of Earth. The moon is about 384,000 km (240,000 miles) away, and it takes a manned spacecraft three days to travel from Earth to the moon.

Fast Facts

- It would take a modern jet fighter more than a million years to reach the nearest star.
- A light year is the distance that light travels in one year.
  It is about 9.5 trillion or 9.5 million million km (6 trillion miles).
- How big is the universe? No one knows, because we can't see the edge of it – if there is one. All we do know is that the visible universe is at least ninety-three billion light years across.
- The universe has no centre.

The History of The Constellations

The constellation system used today stems from the patterns recognised by the ancient Greeks and Roman civilization.

The earliest surviving account of the ancient Greek constellations comes from the poet Aratus of Soli (c 315-245 BC). His poem *Phaenomena,* written about 275 BC, describes the sky in story book fashion and identifies forty-seven constellations.

This poem is based on the lost book of the same name by the Greek astronomer Eudoxus (c 390-340 BC). Eudoxus reputedly introduced the constellations to the Greeks after learning about them from priests in Egypt. These constellations had been adopted from Babylonian culture. They were originally created by the Sumerians around 2000 BC.

Ptolemy, a Greek scientist, arranged them into forty-eight constellations in 150 AD. In about the tenth century AD, an Arab astronomer named al-Sufi updated the *Almagest* in his *Book of Fixed Stars*, which included Arabic names for many stars. These Arabic names are still used today, although often in corrupted form.

No more constellations were introduced until the end of the sixteenth century, when Dutch explorers sailed to the East Indies. From there they could observe the southern sky that was below the European horizon. Two navigators, Pieter Dirkszoon Keyser and Frederick de Houtman, catalogued nearly 200 new southern stars from which their mentor Petrus Placius, a leading Dutch cartographer, created twelve new constellations. Placius also created other northern constellations forming them between those listed by Ptolemy. Nearly a century later, Johannes Hevelius filled the remaining gaps in the northern sky, and in the mid-eighteenth century, the French astronomer Nicolas Louis de Lacaille introduced another fourteen constellations into the southern sky, making it the eighty-eight constellations we now have.

*(Source: **Universe, The definitive Visual Guide** by General Editor Martin Rees)*

Wormholes and Portals

Since the 1930s, physicists have speculated about the existence of wormholes in space.

Wormholes are hypothetical areas of warped spacetime with

Our Ancestors From the Stars

great energy that can create tunnels through spacetime, and if traversable would allow a traveller to quickly move through great distances in space and also travel through time. The difficulty lies in keeping the wormhole open while the traveller makes his journey: if the opening snaps shut, he will never survive to emerge at the other side.

For years, scientists believed that the transit was physically impossible. But recent research, especially by the US physicist Kip Thorne in his book *Black Holes and Timewarps – Einstein's Outrages Legacy* (1994), suggests that: '. . . *it could be done using exotic materials capable of withstanding the immense forces involved. Even then, the time machine would be of limited use – for example, you could not return to a time before the wormhole was created.*

Using wormhole technology would also require a society so technologically advanced that it could master and exploit the energy within black holes.'

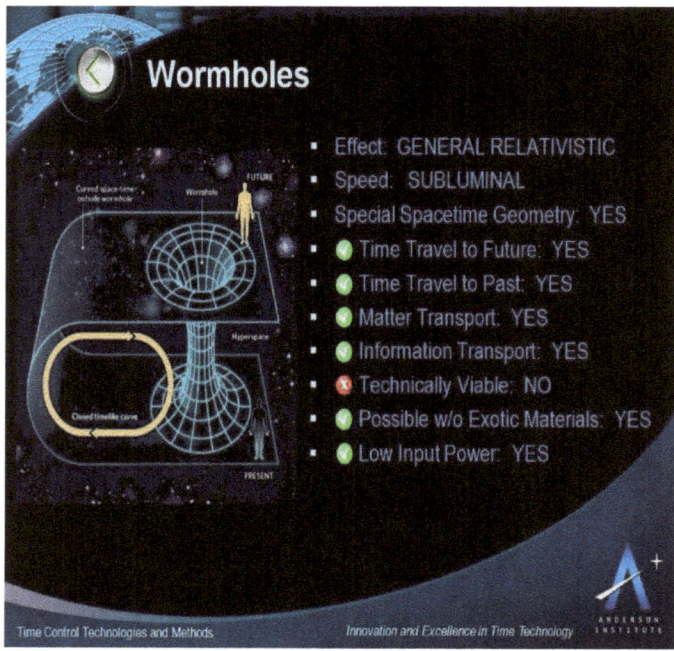

The Seeding of the Stars; The Birth of the Alien Species

Note

I need to emphasize that most of the following information by the people below is a compilation assembled from contactees and channellers obtained from regression sessions, where people went back to past lives on other planets and from active recall by people who started remembering elements of past lives. Understand that those being regressed could have given this information from their own point of view.

With that considered, I have sourced the contents of the following chapters from the work of the people listed below:

Zecharia Stichin: *The 12th Planet:*
https://www.bibliotecapleyades.net/sitchin/planeta12/12planeteng_index.htm#Contents

Wes Penre *Genesis Papers: Human Origins and the living:*
http://wespenre.com/human-origins-and-the-living-library.htm

Humanity's History and Ancient Civilizations:

https://bibliotecapleyades.net/esp_historia_humanidad.htm
Lyssa Royal:
https://www.bibliotecapleyades.net/esp_autor_lyssaroyal.htm
Manuel Lamiroy:

http://www.exopaedia.org/Exopolitics The index on this site has been invaluable to me.

There is an enormous amount of information available from these sites and this is merely a very short synopsis of the overall history of the galactic history.

There are over 10,000,000 worlds in this universe with similar humanities to our own, and the following, mentioned below, are only but a few races that are or have been involved with our lives here on planet Earth over thousands of years.

(Learn about them here: http://www.exopaedia.org/alpha.php)

There are also approximately twenty galactic federations and councils involved in the spiritual evolution of the human race here on planet Earth. It would seem that Ashtar Command, United Federation of Planets, and Andromeda Council, are the ones most frequently mentioned by the contactees.

In the Beginning

In the beginning, about forty or fifty million years ago, the founders created humanoids and placed them in the constellation Lyra. The founders also created other humanoid species on other planets, as well as animal-like species which were also distributed on particular stars in each of the other constellations.

This was the case for all constellations, apart from the inhabitants of the constellation Draco, a reptilian (serpent) race known as Draconians. They are the oldest reptilian race in our universe, and their forefathers came from another separate universe or reality system, but no one knows when, not even the Draconians. Their original home was in the constellation of Draco, the dragon. The Draconians are an androgynous (both male and female) race, and are said to be master geneticists who have created several races. Because of this, they have come to consider themselves as some kind of gods, and have grown an attitude of absolute superiority towards other races.

As mentioned above, the main genetic strains of planet Earth's humanoid consciousness originally began in the constellation Lyra. Lyrian light-skinned, (Nordic) Caucasians, and Lyrian slightly darker skinned (Mediterraneans, Native Americans, East Indians to Aborigines) came from Vega. (Known as Vegans, not because they were vegetarians!) These were also known as the Red Race. These two groups lived peacefully and in harmony on several of the stars for forty million years, and developed agriculture, advanced technologically and scientifically and eventually developed space travel.

Also living in the Lyra constellation was a third humanoid race, on the star Apex, but these were torn apart by duality and conflicts, resulting in the Apex planet nearly self-destructing in a nuclear war. Hardly anyone survived, and those who did had to live underground for several generations, which changed the tone of their skin into grey, and forced their eyes to grow considerably in order to be able to see in the dark. Because of their physical appearance, they are known as Greys. They eventually became the race of the Zeta Reticuli (Zetas).

(Source: Lyssa Royal)

The Draconians who had already established a few bases around the constellations decided to do a bit of pillaging and raping in the constellation of Lyra, thus causing much destruction, which lead to the destruction of many of the planets in that star system. But fortunately, a large number of Lyrians managed to escape and find refuge on certain stars in the following constellations:

Pleiades – a group of stars in Taurus (the bull) where a large group of light skinned (Nordics) predominantly settled.

Tau Ceti – Cetus (the whale).

Procyon – Canis Minor (the lesser dog).

Antaries – Scorpius (the scorpion, but in heraldry also depicted as an eagle).

Alpha Centauri – Centaurus (the centaur).

Bernard Star – Ophiuchus (the serpent bearer).

Arctures – Bootes (the herdsman).

Canis Major – the star Sirius A (the Red Race). This is the brightest star known as the Dog Star (associated with Isis). And Sirius B, of which some are red, brown and black.

The Draconian's main base was on Alpha Draconis, but they had colonies in the following star systems which are under their control:

Orion (associated with Osiris) – Rigel and Bellatrix.

Bootes – Epsilon.

Reticuli – Zeta II, (the Greys), as well as a few minor bases on Capella, Aurig, Ursa Minor and Ursa Mayor.

Below ground and under the oceans are many bases occupied by the above Draconian controlled races including many Grey clones.

The above races are all humanoid in appearance with complexions

which are white, brown, black, red and yellow. Even the reptiles/Draconians look human; it is only their DNA that is different.

June Rye

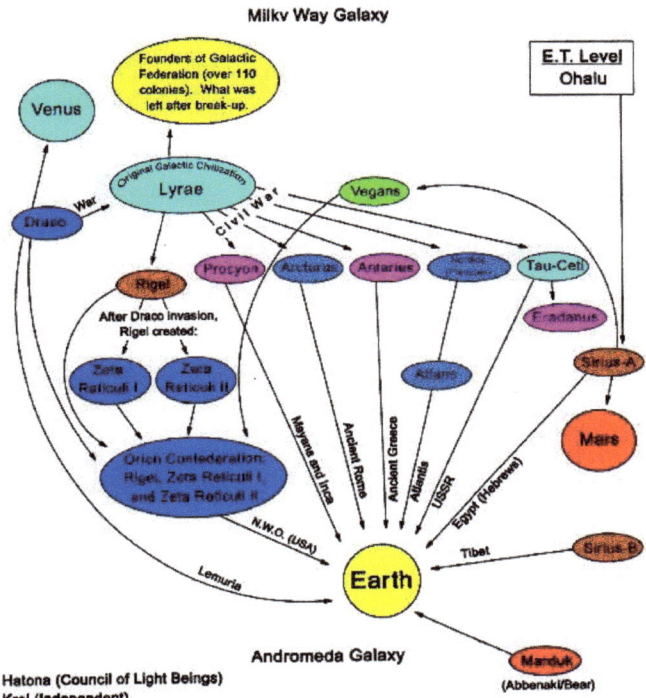

(Source: Stewart Swerdlow)

The species below were not humanoids, but can either show themselves in their original state or at times project themselves as having a human body:

The Carians – the bird people. They have their home in the constellation of Orion. They are the parent race of the reptiles. The genes of the Carians and the Draconians are responsible for the winged serpent of the South American tribes.

The Felines – the lion people. Their home is in the Lyra constellation. They were highly revered by the Egyptians.

The Mantis – these are insectoid beings. They assist, and in many ways, oversee the Zeta Reticulan hybrid program and human spiritual advancement project.

Over millions of years of skirmishes and colonisation, the collective gene pool of the star people acquired a certain amount of Draconian (reptilian) DNA, but significantly more in some species than in others.

Over a few more millions of years, some colonised Venus, Mars, our moon and Maldek, the fifth planet at the time. The remnants of Maldek now make up the asteroid belt between Mars and Jupiter. The story goes that they were so scientifically advanced that one day they accidently set off a hydrogen bomb and the planet was blown to smithereens, thereby killing off most of their population.

In the meantime, about 400 million years ago, when planet Earth was ready to be seeded, the founders gave those species living on Mars instructions to start seeding the planet.

They came periodically to add the many organisms, and they tried the various plant species from their original planet to see which were more suited to grow in Earth's atmosphere. They started experimenting, trying to create animal and aquatic species. (The experiments were started on Mars and the results later transferred to Earth.) It would seem that it was then that the large reptilian and amphibian species were created.

Then, at around 280 million years ago, there was a mass extinction which was caused by some unknown catastrophe. So, they started from scratch again, still trying various DNA strains. But once again an error occurred, which resulted in the creation of a more dinosaur-type species. This is, according to Wes Penre's "Genesis Paper", is when they also started mixing their own DNA with that of the dinosaurs, which over thousands of years evolved into the 'home-grown' reptilian species.

So, we now had the humanoid/Vegan/reptilian hybrids. These had the shape of the humanoid but the mindset (the personality) and DNA of the reptilian. (These were the indigenous reptilians and nothing to do with the Draconians which originated from the constellation Draco.) And with the various species of birds, mammals and seeds of trees, grasses and flowering plants, everything started to become established. Around 66.4 million years ago, the dinosaurs became extinct, but the mammals lived on and starting flourishing. How this happened is a mystery, and some scientists are of the opinion that Earth was hit by a massive planet. But according to Wes Penre in the *Genesis Paper,* 'the big reptiles were intentionally gotten rid of because they were no longer needed, and were too dangerous to have around, so the founders got rid of them.' Perhaps they were nuked?

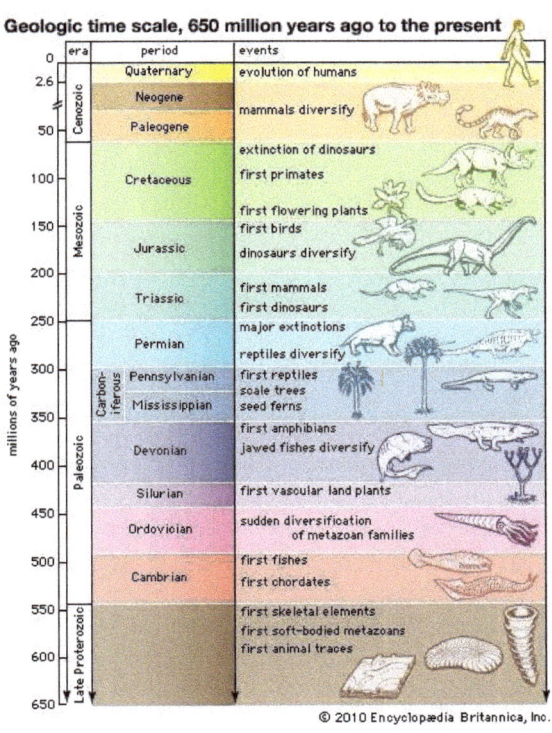

(Source: used with permission of Encyclopædia Britannica, Inc., copyright 2010)

The Ramapithecus seems to be the first. They were around about fifteen to twenty million years ago. They were tree-dwelling, simple tool-users, without visible ancestors or descendants.

About the same time, there was the Australopithecus, but they eventually, and also mysteriously, died out.

In the meantime, in the heavens, galactic star wars were continuously going on, and according to Alex Collier's *Letters from Andromeda,* the Hatona Council from our galaxy convened for many eons as the fighting continued in the Solar System. Finally, with their intercession, an agreement was reached between some of the human factions and the reptilian Earth colonists.

The agreement stated that a new breed of humanity would be created on Earth that would contain the DNA of all interested parties who participated in the 'peace' process, and designated areas on Earth would be set aside for the creation of this new species. The Earth-based reptilians agreed to this under the condition that the reptilian body be the foundation of this new being. Twelve humanoid groups and one reptilian group donated DNA for this purpose. (This explains why ancestors of mankind appear and then suddenly disappear in layers of archaeological analysis.)

So, what does it mean when the original Bible states, 'Let us make man in our own image'? This is a plural statement because it was a group project. (I assume that it was at this stage – about three to four million years ago – when the genetic tinkering started taking place.) And why is the first man in the Bible is also called Adam? As we've discussed, the name Adam comes from the Hebrew 'Adama' meaning 'created of Earth's soil, or Sumerian 'Adapa' meaning 'model man'. He was a crossbreed of genes of Earth's primates and the group of extraterrestrials responsible for the creation of the white, yellow, red, brown and black races who are the inhabitants of our planet.

It should be remembered that the following ET species have been around for millions of years, and have interbred with some and been colonised by others in our galaxy and have, by now, developed into their present appearance, personalities and various blood groups. They were from the species living on Mars, also Vega, Lyra, Sirius, Pleiadian, Orion (whose DNA was partly Draconian), the Nibiru tribe (the Anunnaki), and the Earth-based reptilians of Lumeria (the humanoid/Vegan reptilian hybrids) who agreed to this under the condition that the reptilian body be the foundation of this new being.

At that time the atmosphere on Mars was similar to that of Earth and there were several species of ETs living on Mars. (See *Mars – The Lost History of Man*: http://talc.site88.net/mars.php.) This is obviously not the case now, but it is thought that several extraterrestrials have an underground basis there (and the moon) at present, and have had for hundreds of years.

Around 3.5 million years ago, Homo habilis appeared. He was an upright, tool-using, hunting, home-dwelling being who looked much like proto-humans – although definite ancestral links to us have not yet been established.

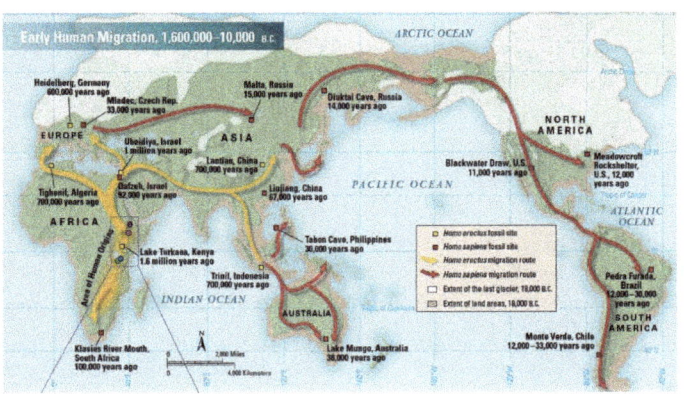

Homo erectus came roughly between 750,000 and 250,000 years ago. He was a stone axe-user, a fire-kindler and hut-builder, with a brain somewhat comparable to ours. The females no longer went 'on heat' (oestrus), and offspring went through a much more prolonged infancy. Cultural growth was beginning, and signs of humanity were evident.

There is no demonstrated relationship between Homo erectus and Homo neanderthalis, who appears about 300,000 years ago, wearing clothes, practicing ritual burials and warfare, but who also mysteriously and quickly disappeared some 35,000 years BC. The Neanderthals displayed virtually no technological innovation during more than 100,000 years of their existence on the planet, and they just disappeared (they were not killed off by Cro-Magnons). They didn't interbreed either. Modern humans are not descended from Neanderthals, but co-existed with them about 40,000 years ago according to the latest scientific research just recently released.

Various 'Edens'

After much searching, I feel that the DNA tweaking must have begun from about 900,000 in the various Edens below. (I am using the dates from Alex Collier's *An Andromedan Perspective on Galactic History*: http://www.alexcollier.org/alex-collier-history-of-the-galaxy-2002/)

I personally think it's quite feasible to assume that while the above hunter-gatherers were going about their business populating the planet according to the above early human migration map (1,600.000–10,000 BC), the various ET races (including the Anunnaki) were living amongst them busy adapting the earthling's genes, building pyramids, and vast complexes such as Gobekli Tepe and the stone circles, and leaving little clues all over the place for us to find, dig up and ponder about when the time was right – which is obviously now, at the beginning of this age. The following is a list of the various Edens:

763,132 BC: CHINA in the province of Shaanxi – This is where the Orion group founded their first Eden. On Google Earth, there is a cluster of huge earthen pyramids lying about seven miles south-east of Xi'an City in China. It surely can't be a coincidence that this particular group is aligned to the *same stars* in Orion's Belt as the Great Pyramid of Giza and Teotihuacan in Mexico? (See 'Pyramid Power'.)

74l,237 BC: Chile – A group from Capella (Aurig), Ursa Major and Ursa Minor, establish their Eden at the base of Mt Yogan in southern Chile.

70l,655 BC: Libyan/Niger border – The Vegans (from Lyra) who are the humans with the darker Mediterranean complexion. I ask myself, *could this possibly be where the Dravidian's of India originally evolved from and perhaps the Algerian and some of the Arab nations*?

604,003 BC: Algeria/North Africa – Colonised by the Cassiopeias. This is an entirely insectoid sentient race.

585,133 BC: Cairo, Egypt – Colonised by the Orion/Sirius group. (Remember Osiris and Isis?) It would seem that at the same time Orion sent a team to **Perth, Australia**.

445,000 BC: Eridu, Persian Gulf (Sumerian/Sitchin) – This was the first place the Anunnaki settled in. They set up an unsuccessful gold mining operation there and later moved their headquarters to **Nippur** in **Mesopotamia, Iraq**, and later to **Zimbabwe** in **Southern Africa**.

This is the crucial point from which the Orion/Sirius ET race, the Anunnaki from Nibiru, seriously started creating the indigenous human race in Africa, first as slave labour to mine their gold, and then later with the cooperation and donated DNA from various other star nations. Consequently we, the human race, have, over thousands of years, evolved into our present selves.

The Anunnaki

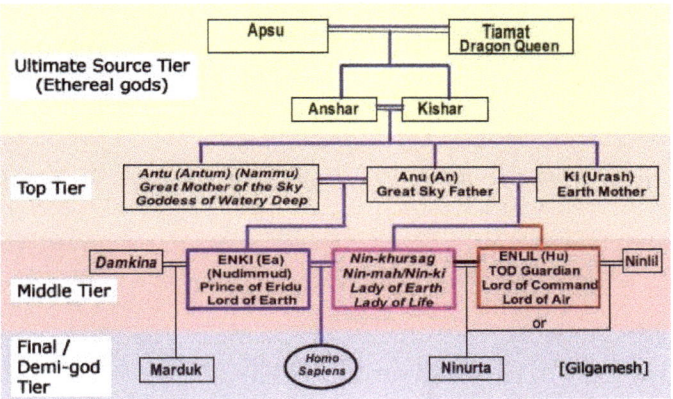

The Family Tree and History of the Anunnaki Orion/Sirian Tribe

Let us now look at some more information on the creation of the tribe known as the 'Anunnaki':

For millions of years, war raged between the male-dominated human/reptilian species from Sirius and the female-dominated human/reptilian constellation of Orion. Eventually an agreement was reached to end the war and they decided to combine their colonies. A marriage was then arranged between Queen Antu[1] and King Anu.

---

[1] Queen Antu did not need a sexual partner to have children. If she needed to give birth to a son, she kept her egg unfertilized. If she wanted a daughter she fertilised the egg herself. This is called Parthenogenesis – a method used by some species of fish, birds and reptiles. Also note that Enki's genes are pure Orion. This is obvious from the fact that he wanted the human race to have knowledge, thus the temptation of Eve with the Apple. (Interesting too is the thought of Mary and the virgin birth of Jesus. Could she too have been an Anunnaki from Orion?)

After a few thousand years, there was a split and a large group, led by their children Enki and Enlil (they were half-brothers), and their sister Ninkhursac, moved and settled on Nibiru (Planet X) according to Alex Collier.

After a few more thousand years, when they found they had depleted Nibiru of its mineral content by experimenting with nuclear power, they went off in search of minerals, especially gold, and eventually landed up in Sumeria (Iraq) on planet Earth.

It was the Sumerian people who called them Anunnaki, which translates into 'Those who from heaven to Earth came'. Nibiru, according to scientists, is the twelfth planet in our solar system, and is located somewhere beyond Pluto.

It is generally believed that the Anunnaki were the first alien species to make contact with Earth according to the Sumerian tablets. But they were not the first. As I mentioned before, various species of ETs have been involved in our planet for millions of years: at first preparing it for the eventual habitation for a human species, and eventually living on it, each creating their 'Edens' in various places until the creator gods were satisfied with each prototype of Adam in the various races, resulting in the black, brown, yellow, red and white people of our planet.

The Anunnaki were the first beings who left clear written proof on clay tablets about how the first black human race was created and lived in Africa.

These tablets were discovered in 1849, and the content only made public in 1976 by the Hebrew scholar Zecharia Sitchin who decoded the Sumerian cuneiform script. But it was not until the early 2000s that this information was suddenly being written about. (I should point out that these tablets with the message contained within them were purposely hidden until the human race had matured enough to be able to handle this very important information about how we were created by using extraterrestrial genes. This information was hidden just like the Rosetta Stone, which was 'discovered' in Egypt in 1799.)

What follows is the story of the Anunnaki which was translated from the Sumerian clay tablets, not only by Zecharia Sitchin, but subsequently by various other scholars:

About 445,000 to 360,000 years ago, the Anunnaki came in their space ships with 600 workers (according to the Sumerian tablets) with the intention of mining gold and other minerals on Earth. They eventually settled in Sumeria. Enlil was given Northern Africa to look after, and Enki Southern Africa, below the equator. Enki was also known as the creator god, and was the serpent who tempted Eve with the apple.

At first, their own people mined the gold, but the workers realised this was too much work and started rebelling, so Enki and Enlil decided to call on their sister Ninkhursag, who was chief medical officer, to come and help them with a little cloning and DNA tweaking. This was done by mixing their own DNA with that of Earth's Homo erectus and subsequently creating, through trial and error, the Adams and Eves of the indigenous African race. This took a few hundred years. (Remember, there were many other prototypes of Adams being created by various other alien species in different regions of the planet. (See 'Human DNA' and 'Giants'.)

Many scholars, after carefully analysing the Sumerian tablets, are now coming to the conclusion that the stories written on the them about this creation and the continual skirmishes with neighbours, tie up exactly with the stories written in the Old Testament about the wars between the Israelites and their neighbours.

The book *African Temples of the Anunnaki* (2013) by Michael Tellinger was an absolute gift from the gods to me! He documents thousands of circular stone ruins, monoliths, ancient roads, agricultural terraces, and prehistoric mines in South Africa, and reveals how these 200,000-year-old sites perfectly match Sumerian descriptions of Abzu, the land of the First People – including the vast gold mining operations of the Anunnaki from the twelfth planet, Nibiru, and the city of the Anunnaki leader Enki. I have his permission to quote from the chapter 'Human Origins and Mythology':

> *'When we realize that most of the stories from Genesis to Exodus are translations from their original source written in the Sumerian tablets, it all starts to make a lot of sense. The same gods that the Sumerian tablets refer to are the same plural gods that are mentioned in the Bible. All the greatest stories have their origins in the Sumerian tablets.*
>
> *While the story is often reduced to one line in the Bible, the original Sumerian texts are written in much greater detail: The seven tablets of creation of heaven and Earth; creation of Adamu, the biblical Adam; creation of Eve from Adamu's rib; the garden of Eden; the serpent and the tree of knowledge and life; the Flood: Noah (Ziusudra) and the ark; the destruction of Sodom and Gomorrah; the tower of Babel and its destruction by the gods, and many more. These tales are all well documented by the Sumerians and some of these tablets predate the Bible by as much as 3,000 years.'*

It should also be noted that Enlil was Jehovah (YHWH), the god of the Old Testament and the Qu'ran, and Enki (Enlil's half-brother), the creator god who was also the serpent in the garden who wanted mankind to acquire the gift of knowledge.

We shall now leave the subject of the Anunnaki and their southern African mining and human genetic experimental projects, as these continued for several thousands of years until the flood, and discuss what the other extraterrestrial races had been doing:

87,300 BC: Perth, Australia – Orion establishes another colony there.

83,400 BC: Basque Country – We are told the Lyrans came back, which obviously indicates that they had been there before and that the native language spoken in that country is an ancient Lyran tongue that has survived.

73,414 BC: Mt Neblina – The Orion's revisit their settlement on the border of Venezuela and Brazil.

But there were other events, too, and we shall now discuss the lost continents of Atlantis and Lemuria.

Atlantis

I read somewhere that over 500 books have been written about Atlantis, and when I Googled Atlantis in the Bibliotecapleyades. net site, every time asking a slightly different question about Atlantis, about twelve sites popped up giving the basic story – but with reams of contradictory material. Much was written about Enki (the serpent god) from Sumeria and his role in their affairs, but I prefer not to get too involved in that story as the purpose of this section is to give a brief story about the history of Atlantis.

Atlantis – The lost continent: an artist's depiction of the location of Atlantis according to Plato

We first hear about Atlantis from the Greek philosopher Plato, who told the story around 360 BC. He said the founders of Atlantis were half-god half-human, and that they created a utopian civilization and became a great naval power. Their home was made up of concentric islands separated by wide moats and linked by a canal that penetrated to the centre. The lush islands contained gold, silver and other precious metals and supported an abundance of exotic wild life. There was a great capital city on the central island.

According to the Salem New Age Centre's 1998 *Ancient Earth History Civilization Time Line,* Atlantis makes an appearance around 400,000 BC. (It is interesting to note that this was the time the Anunnaki started mining gold and creating slaves in Mesopotamia and Southern Africa.)

Edgar Cayce (Mystic and Prophet)) mentions a highly advanced civilization that flourished in the Atlantic Ocean in 200,000 BC, and according to him the Atlantians were well-versed in technology that harvested the power of the quantum world, and this included the use of crystals and sound waves for healing. Elevators and connecting tunnels were operated with compressed air and steam, and Atlantians were adept at the use of silicon chips at levels unrivalled in the modern world, and were familiar with the amplification power of crystals in laser technology and memory chips. (Today's cell/mobile phone is watered down Atlantian technology.) They also perfected the use of sound to elevate massive stone blocks for the construction of buildings, in particular the temples. A genetic engineering team used crystals and quartz in huge quantities when they created and manipulated life forms in their laboratories, where many strange things happened: experiments of non-physical life forms taking animal bodies, or bodies that were half-human half-animal, for example. There were also experiments with genetic manipulation and cloning, leading to a race of 'human machines'.

Let's look at some other dates to do with Atlantis:

Around 50,700-50,000 – the start of the time period of huge Earth changes due to a shift of the magnetic poles of the earth. Atlantis lost land and became an archipelago of five islands. According to Cayce, the first destruction of a portion of Atlantis appears to have been caused 'accidentally' by explosives that were used improperly, triggering volcanic action. That is the time when the first emigrations out of Atlantis occurred. People migrated to the areas of the Pyrenees, Portugal, Spain, Egypt and the Americas.

20,000-10,500 BC – conflict gradually arose between the scientific and technological leaders against the philosopher group who wanted to enlighten the sub-being creations by raising their consciousness. Cayce also mentions that before the final deluge, some Altantians who managed to escape to Egypt buried an archive of their civilisation's history and accomplishments under one the Sphinx's paws.

Recently, there has been further research conducted around the Sphinx with new technology. During one of the Discovery Channel's specials, researchers confirmed that they could, in fact, see a room under the left paw of the Sphinx. However, the Egyptian director of antiquities would not allow excavations in that area for any reason.

(Source: https://www.historicmysteries.com/edgar-cayce-atlantis/ and www.exopaedia.org/Atlantis)

Lemuria (Mu)

Lemuria was a continent located in the Pacific Ocean and a cultural period that predated and overlapped Atlantis.

The search for Lemuria has not been an easy one as there were many views and timelines from which to try and make any sense of events. It was interesting to find that apart from the ET races mentioned below, Lemuria was also the home of the serpent gods, the Kumaras (the name means 'androgynous serpents'). This particular group originated from the constellation Draco, having first settled on the planet Venus before moving to Lemuria.

This is how dates of Lemuria differ:
- According to Edgar Cayce, the Christian mystic, Lemuria was established in the Pacific Ocean in 900,000 BC. It was destroyed in 500,000 BC, and was restored in 350,000, before finally disappearing in 250,000 BC.
- David Childress, author and specialist in ancient archaeology, however, puts the date at 78,000 years ago.
- James Churchward, an occult writer, indicates it disappeared between 50,000 to 12,000 years ago.

- According to Alex Collier, who has documented his contact with alien beings, Lemuria was founded as a collective colony in the Pacific in 71,933 BC, and inhabited by the following star nations: Lyrans, Pleiades (specifically Teygeta and Merope Stars), Alpha Centauri, and Sirius.

As a civilization, Lemuria presented a feminine energy, purity of heart and emotions, and a simple yet deep connection with divinity. They worshiped the sun and lived in tune with nature. They were visited by other, more advanced, species, and learned scientific technology from them, particularly in the building of megalithic buildings that were able to withstand earthquakes. There were many skirmishes between Lemuria (Mu) and Atlantis, which was ruled by a patriarchal society.

Lemuria was the birthplace of spiritual healing groups such as the Solar Brotherhood of the Children of the Sun, as well as the Solar Brotherhood of the Seven Rays, and the Great White Brotherhood. They are known by different names by various nations, but they basically stem from the same original spiritual healing group, whose forefathers were known as the Kumaras.

I found the map below on Google Images and fortunately, after many weeks of searching, eventually found the story behind this particular map. It shows the islands which survived the Great Flood, or deluge.

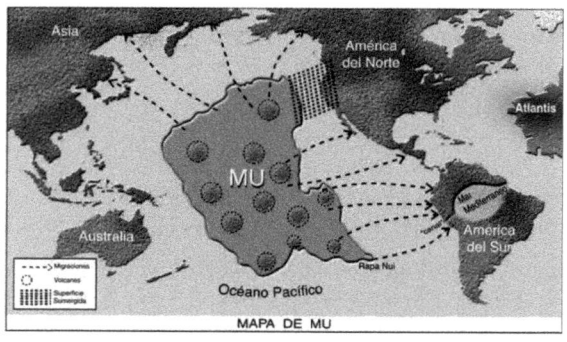

(Copyright: Antön Ponce de Leön Paiva)

I have been corresponding with Mr Antön Ponce de Leon, who is a pioneer of investigating extraterrestrial life in Peru, and a writer and international lecturer specialising in cosmovision and Andean spirituality. He is also the founder of the Solar Brotherhood of the Children of the Sun in Peru. In his first book "*The Wisdom of the Ancient ONE*" he tells the story of his initiation and his second – "*In Search of the Wise ONE*" he writes of his search way back to his teacher.

His first sighting of a UFO occurred in 1938 when he was seven years old. He writes about this experience as follows: *'It was one winter's night in 1938 when I was seven years old, walking in the mountains of the Sacred Valley of the Incas-Cusco-Peru with my father when I saw a "flying saucer" – the term UFO did still not exist. For me it looked like a "star walking" through the sky. For my father and the several Quechua peasants accompanying him this was not a strange phenomenon. The Map of Mu that appears in my third published book (I have four edited in several languages) was received telepathically and approved by my teacher Quechua Amaru Cusi Yupanqui.'*

These Elders who are the direct descendants of the Incas and high priests of the Inca Empire have lived in the secret hidden village within the Andes since the downfall of that civilization. The map shows that Mu (Lemuria) was once connected to North America, approximately at Mount Shasta, located in Northern California, and the circles on the map indicate the Pacific islands which survived the cataclysm. Australia, New Zealand, the Pacific Islands, Japan, the Philippines and Hawaii are all remnants of Lemuria.

Here I must admit I am rather confused, because the information below seems to apply to Noah's flood, but legend also tells me that Lemuria sank a few thousand years before Atlantis; but on the other hand, there is evidence of the underground cities mentioned in the chapter 'Ancient Underground Tunnels', so I shall stick with the deluge story of around 10,000 BC.

The legend goes that these holy people, the serpent lords, received information that in approximately 2,000-3,000 years' time the earth was to experience a cataclysmic event. A meeting was held and Sanat Kumara, chief of the serpent lords, elected the lords who were to start storing information about the history of mankind in crystals which were to be hidden in various parts of the planet. They were told to make use of the underground tunnels that existed between power points of the planet, and start establishing underground cities in various locations around the planet. Approximately a year before the impending disaster, they gathered communities together and took them underground to prepare them for living in that environment.

The deluge came, and after the water receded the people emerged from under the ground and saw that everything had changed. This emergence from the earth is the point at which the myths of this flood and the creation of the various nations began. In a very literal sense, they did emerge from the earth, and most of the native peoples had lost the exact memories of this emergence; but within the highest ranks of the shamans, this knowledge is still passed on. (See 'The Identity of the Serpent Gods'.)

(More information about Lemuria (MU) on: http://wespenre.com/2/shamans-of-mu-fallen-angels-and-corruption-of-wisdom.htm)

The Anunnaki in Africa and the Pleiades

Let's go back to the Anunnaki in Africa. The creation and cloning of workers for the mines in Africa was going well, but then Enki, being the scientist he was, wanted to expand his creation even further by adding an extra set of genes to our DNA, so he visited the Pleiades – also known as Nordics – who had white skin, blond hair and blue eyes, and were also exceptionally tall, some of them being up to eight feet tall.

(Source: http://wespenre.com/2/shamans-of-mu-fallen-angels-and-corruption-of-wisdom.htm Scroll down to 8 "A Gigantic visit from the Pleiades")

There were many pitfalls with the various experiments with DNA, which is evident from all the skeletons that have been found with deformities such as extra rows of teeth, four or six fingers on the hands, and elongated skulls, to name just a few. As expected, it took many decades and countless experiments here on Earth to create the perfect race. The offspring of this experiment became the biblical Nephilim.

Once the Pleiadian genetic experiments took off, giants of all sizes started to roam Earth, and it is said that in the beginning these enormous creatures coexisted quite well with the already existing humans and didn't bother them too much. The population grew and Enlil, although not happy with Enki's new creation, did however use giants in different kinds of missions, often as a police force or military force. Some of them, who had more Sirian genes than others, were quite aggressive, and eventually descended into cannibalism; while others were mellower and began a positive relationship with humans. Enki picked out some of the wisest and most trustworthy of the Nephilim to rule kingdoms in certain parts of the world.

It would seem the Enki and Ninharsag were greatly inspired to experiment after the Pleiadians came, and humans were once again crossed with humans and animals (this had previously been done in Atlantis), but this time in other, more unpleasant ways. One could see human bodies with bull heads, bird heads and other grotesque abnormalities.

From what I can gather, by around 11,000 BC, the world had not only become overpopulated with various races (some of them giants), but there were also many unsuccessful prototypes roaming parts of the world. King Anu and the queen of the Orion empire (parents of Enki and Enlil) watched their former paradise turn into a cosmic zoo with a lot of abominable beings wandering aimlessly about, eating each other and also killing and eating humans. For many thousands of years, they had left Enki alone because they knew that if they interfered, Enki would kill off his creation and also the creations of the other star nations. But it had come to the point that something drastic had to be done.

(Source: http://wespenre.com/4/paper14-antediluvian-times-and-utnapishtims-heavenly-ark.htm)

A meeting was held somewhere in Orion, and to cut a long story short, it was decided that they should get rid of everything and start again. Over the following thousand years, they sent a plague and then a drought, but that still left a large number of people on Earth. It was then finally agreed that Enlil would cause a deluge, and it was agreed that the humans would not be warned, and an oath was sworn by everybody present.

(Source: http://wespenre.com/genes-of-isis.htm)

The Great Flood

The Great Deluge

This was a *very* important time in history, as the Anunnaki started to hide records and computer programs deep in the Iraqi soil. They also prepared genetic banks of Earth's creatures to save them from the coming flood. They then collected female eggs and the female essence (samples of the female DNA code), therefore all the living kind to combine. Then they waited for the flood.

But Enki secretly told Noah (his son by an earthling) to build a submersible boat and take the DNA library of all the species of the planet, together with his immediate family, and live in the submarine until the waters subsided. Enki then shut down the gold mines in South Africa and prepared to leave. In Atlantis, however, some also heard about an impending catastrophe and many fled, including a group of giants, to South America. Some hid in underground caves, and other high up in the Andes. The Anunnaki left in their space ships, some to Mars; while others hovered above the earth until the storm subsided.

I found three theories explaining this particular flood:

- Geologists agree that there was indeed a cataclysmic occurrence involving floods and earthquakes in an epoch of great global instability between 10,800 BC and 9600 BC.
- A meteorite crashed into the ice cap and caused the deluge.
- According to Edgar Cayce (*The Sleeping Prophet*), the people of Atlantis had constructed laser-like crystals for power plants, and these were responsible for the final destruction of the land, thus causing the deluge.

After the Deluge

Eventually, when the oceans subsided and the survivors came out of their hiding places, they found the dead bodies of thousands of humans, animals and other creatures floating off shore. Understandably chaos broke out: people started fighting amongst themselves trying to find food; and some organised themselves in groups and armed themselves with whatever they could find to protect themselves, most of all from the giants, some of whom had survived.

This catastrophic event sent shockwaves through the star nations of the galaxy, and various star nation's ETs came down to help rectify the situation. They organised the nations back into their various tribes, and it is from this point in time that the stories about the flood and the creation of the individual nations eventually became myths. For example, myths developed that the serpent gods of the South American nations, the Far East, India and Africa, came out of the ground, and some gods came down in chariots from the sky. It is interesting that these mythical stories all feature in the flood and creation myths in every nation on the planet. Below are a few examples:
- ~ **Lung** (dragons) in China.
- ~ **Djedhi** (snakes) in Egypt.
- ~ **Quetzalcoatl** (plumed serpents) in Mexico.

- ~ **Nagas** (snakes) in India.

And in Australia, the aboriginal people have carefully preserved legends of the serpent in there so-called 'dreamtime' myths of Earth's creation, and so on.

It is only in the Christian Bible that the serpent is depicted as a force of evil, and as noted before, this particular serpent (Enki, our creator) was the one who tempted Eve to eat the apple from the Tree of Knowledge. (Amusing to note that the Apple computer logo is a bitten apple!)

It is from this point that the various ET civilisations established themselves all over the planet again: the Tiahuanacan culture in the mountainous plateau between Bolivia and Peru in South America established the cities of Tiahunaco and Punku; others were established in Baalbek in Lebanon; Nan Madol in Micronesia; Axum and Lilabela in Ethiopia; Dwarka in India; and Yonaguni in Japan.

And the involvement of Orion is significantly clear by the placing of the following three pyramids: Xi'an in China, Teolihuacon in Mexico and Giza in Egypt, which are all in alignment with each other as well the constellation of Orion. (See 'Pyramid Power'.)

(Source: https://www.bibliotecapleyades.net/ciencia/historia_humanidad62.htm)

It would seem from Dolores Cannon (1931-2014), a past life regressionist and hypnotherapist who specialised in past knowledge, that it was around this time that Stonehenge was also constructed.

It was her understanding that it took an unimaginable amount of time for life to be re-established and to thrive. Stored DNA was used to recreate animal and human life, and as humans eventually developed greater intelligence, extraterrestrials assisted in advancing their skills, teaching them to make tools, hunt, and make fire. This enabled early humans once again to form civilisations.

She feels that these extraterrestrials stayed for a very long time, and were treated as gods and goddesses such was their superior intelligence – thus the legends of gods and goddesses were born. As humans became more self-sufficient, they began to return home, but not before knowledge was shared with those able to grasp such and be able to convey this valuable information. She also believes that the extraterrestrials interbred with humans before they left, creating individuals with greater intelligence and abilities, able to lead and develop these civilisations – the business and technological influencers of today. (See 'The Illuminati'.)

The Anunnaki after the Deluge

The following is a brief description of how the Anunnaki coped with the aftermath of this cataclysmic event.

After the deluge, the Anunnaki heard that due to the events on Earth, Nibiru's protective gold shield had once again been ripped off. All the hundreds of thousands of years of effort from the gods and human slaves had been in vain, and the production had to start all over again, just when they thought they had been at the end of the process. But the African mines were gone, the slave workers had drowned, most of the Anunnaki had gone home to Nibiru before the deluge, and the rocket terminal in Sippar, Mesopotamia, was destroyed as well.

Scouts were sent around the planet and reported back that they had found an abundance of gold in Peru, high up in the Andes from modern La Paz and east of Lake Poopo. The gold was in the sand, brought by the water that was running into the east coast of Lake Titicaca. They were also able to combine copper and tin and create bronze (remnants of these ancient mining activities can still be found, both by Lake Titicaca and La Paz).

In the meantime, the Anunnaki kingship was re-established, so King Anu dedicated four major regions to four different groups:

Region 1: Enlil's lineage's domain – Enlil and his lineage, decreed the king, were to rule Mesopotamia through their designated kings, descendants of Ziasudra's sons, Shem and Japhet the Fair. Ziasudra's eldest son, Shem (Šem), and his descendants, were to rule the nations from the highlands running from the Persian Gulf to the Mediterranean. Around 3800 BC, Shem's descendants settled the ex-spaceport area of Iraq and the landing place at Lebanon. Shem's brother Japhet rules for the Enlilites from the highlands of Asia Minor, the Black and Caspian Seas, as well as the nearby coasts and islands, as they recover from the flood.

Region 2: Enki's lineage's domain – King Anu orders Enki and his descendants to rule Egypt and Africa though the descendants of (Ziasudra) Noah's sons, Ham the Dark. Ham's line rules Canaan, Cush, Mizraïm, Nubia, Ethiopia, Egypt and Libya, beginning from the highlands and spreading to the reclaimed lowlands.

Region 3: Inanna's domain – Inanna, Anu instructed, would rule the Indus Valley as a grain source for the other regions.

Region 4: Ninharsag's domain – The forth region, Tilmun (Sinai), Anu declared, should be ruled directly by Ninharsag and be reserved exclusively for Nibiruans and their immediate descendants.

The Anunnaki got on with reseeding their part of the earth. They taught the new humans agriculture. The Tigris and Euphrates rivers were made navigable, and fish were introduced to the waters. Reeds were planted that could be used for building materials. Moving from the seas and rivers to dry land, Enki introduced the people to the plough and the yoke and taught them agriculture, animal husbandry, brick-making and construction of dwellings.

The gods then built the cities of Edin (Mesopotamia), and in each city they built a temple where humans could worship their gods. Ninurta got Lagash, where he got hangars for his aircraft and armoury for his missiles. (He may well have been one of the gods who taught humankind about warfare, being Enlil's 'warrior son'.) Utu, who rebuilt the city of Sippar, taught law to the humans, and Nannar was given the city of Urim. Iškur returned from the Andes to reside in a temple in the mountains north of Mesopotamia (Sumer). Marduk and Nabu, his son, came over to stay with Ea in Eridu.

For many thousands of years, the Anunnaki ruled and squabbled with each other, and having established various tribes used the humans to fight their battles for them. (This is best described in all the Bible stories in the Old Testament.) King Anu (Enki and Elil's father) decided by 2064 BC it was time the Anunnaki gave kingship to the earthlings, because they had enough gold to shield Nibiru's atmosphere so they could all go back to their home.

Then Anu came down to Earth in his spaceship and called a meeting so that everybody could hear:

'If destiny is that mankind is going to take over and rule the world, let it so be. Give them knowledge up to a measure; secrets of heaven and Earth them teach; let them learn about laws and righteousness, then depart and leave.'

Nuclear War

By the end of their stay on Earth, the Anunnaki tried to end all their old feuds with each other, perhaps so as not to take these conflicts back to Nibiru. The humans were used as slave labour to dig up the last gold resources and precious metals and stones needed, and had to them help out with other things, too. Not the least, they had human armies fight wars and battles between the gods to settle things between rival parties. And many rival parties there were.

So, the leaders gathered the Anunnaki council to discuss the matter. All council members were against Marduk and Nabu, and saw them as a major problem in all camps. Most of the Anunnaki on Earth were eager to leave and go home, but before they did, they decided that if Marduk would be the ruler of Earth, at least they should deny him the spaceport in Sinai. All senior Anunnaki, except Ea, agreed to use nuclear weapons to stop Nabu's advance through Canaan towards the Sinai spaceport.

Airships were sent down to bring the Igigi (Anunnaki workers) home. In 2064 BC, Ninurta attacked the Sinai. The first missile hit Mt Mashu, where the controlling equipment was housed. Then, a nuclear bomb was dropped above the place of the celestial rocket ships, with the brilliance of seven suns. The Earth shook and crumbled, the heavens were darkened after the attack, and all of the beautiful forests were destroyed, leaving only burnt stems left.

Nergal, Enki's son, bombed Marduk's forces in Canaan. He nuked Sodom and Gomorrah, and three other cities allied with Marduk. These nukes were what made the Dead Sea dead, and it still hasn't recovered in today's twenty-first century. There is still radioactivity in the area today, enough to induce sterility in animals and people who absorb the water there. Archaeologists have confirmed the flooding, abandonment of the area, and sudden deadening of life in 2024 BC. The destruction was tremendous.

And with that, most of the Anunnaki left the planet, just as destructively as they once arrived.

The above is but a brief description of the events which happened at that time. To get the full story I suggest you log on to the following site http://wespenre.com/after-the-deluge.htm

The Gene Map of the Nations

The following chart shows how the human nations have evolved from the various star nations into their individual groups since this time:

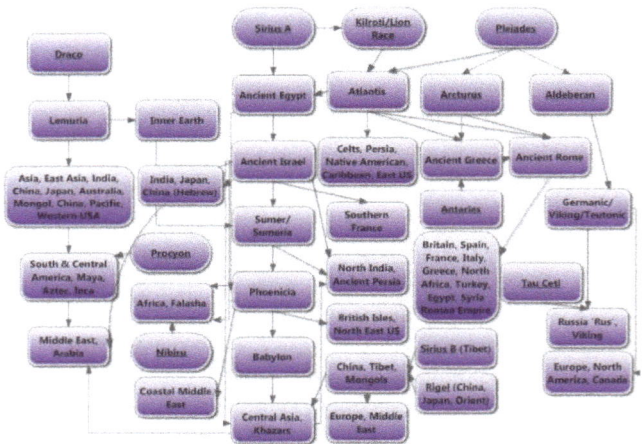

Flow Chart of Galactic Civilisations – Janet and Stewart Swerdlow – *True World History: Humanity's Saga.*

(Source: by permission of Expansion Publishing Company)

Identity of the Gods

Unravelling the Gods

Trying to unravel the names of literally hundreds of named gods on the internet was not an easy task, so imagine my delight when I eventually discovered a site which explained that there were only twelve basic senior gods and goddesses. (There were, of course, many lesser gods and goddesses, but here I am only concerned with the big guys.)

To get the full story of where and when the belief in gods first started, we must go back to the Anunnaki from Nibiru (Planet X) who came to Earth with a team of workers around 445,000 BC to mine gold, but when their Anunnaki workers rebelled, decided to create a human race of workers by mixing their human/reptilian DNA with that of the Neanderthal species who were living on Earth at that time. *I need to emphasize that they did not look like reptiles. It is their reptilian DNA gene which contains the domineering/ambitious part of their makeup.* (See: 'Human DNA'.)

It was this group of extraterrestrials who presented themselves as gods in the first place – and understandably so, don't you think. They came out of the sky in shiny spaceships, and those frightened earthlings most definitely must have thought of these strange people as gods – and these highly advanced extraterrestrial beings would certainly have thought themselves that. Just imagine a UFO arriving in the middle of the bush amongst a tribe of Neanderthals sitting around chipping away at a pile of flint stones! That would certainly have caused an astonishing, if not terrifying, situation. And it would be exactly the same now for those who have not yet experienced this very same phenomena.

I should add here that it was previously mentioned that there were other alien groups who came to Earth and seeded the human race in many variations, but the Anunnaki were the only ones who left written proof of their history from the time of their arrival on the planet in 445,000 BC until their departure in around 2064 BC.

These stories, or myths, first started off with the Nibiruan gods of Anu, Antu, Ninkhursag, and Ishkur. They then became Anshar, Apsu, Ninmah and Adad in Sumerian. In Greek, they became Kronos, Rhea, Hera, and Ares. In Latin, they became Saturn, Ops, Juno and Mars. You will find that the names and point of view changes, but their attributes are virtually identical. We will talk more about this later after the serpent gods.

It has been a tremendous struggle to compile some sort of chronological timeline from the many myths and the stories from the clay tablets and the Bible stories in the Old Testament. One of the greatest problems was because the biblical fraternity in the past has not been able to agree on a date for Noah's flood until now. New literary and archaeological evidence has now been established, as we've mentioned, by Dr David Livingston, who claims that Noah's flood occurred about 2900 BC.

(Source: http://www.davelivingston.com/flooddate.htm)

The following is purely my own thoughts based on the research I have done for the purpose of this book, and to cut a long story short, this is briefly what happened after the deluge which occurred between 10,800 and 9600 BC which caused the end of most of the planet's inhabitants.

Fortunately, the DNA samples of all the Earth's fauna, flora and human DNA had been saved by the various Noah's, and eventually human creation started up again; but this time, the human DNA recipes had already been perfected, so all that was needed was to find suitable land in the Middle East, the Americas (north and south), India, East Asia, Africa, Europe and Australia to start the whole process of seeding the planet from scratch again.

It seems clear to me that it is from this specific time in history, after things had to a certain extend settled down after the flood, that most of the ancient cultures around the world can trace their roots back to the serpent gods.

The Identity of the Serpent Gods

Historically, serpents and snakes represent fertility or a creative life force. As snakes shed their skin through sloughing, they are symbols of rebirth, transformation, immortality and healing. The ouroboros, a circular symbol depicting a snake, or less commonly a dragon swallowing its tail, is an emblem of wholeness or infinity.

Serpent gods are not just found in the history or mythology of the ancient Middle East. Dragons, flying serpents and serpent gods appear in the mythology of people throughout the world, and everywhere are the creators and benevolent ancestors of man. In some cultures, however, there also remains the lingering memory of a serpent race that was cruel and barbaric.

It is interesting to note that it is only in the Torah and the Bible, in the Old Testament, that the snake is depicted as an evil force. The reason for this is the original conflict between the two brothers Enki, (known as the 'Great Serpent') who created us and his brother Enlil (known as Jehovah, YHWH and Allah of the Qur'an). When Enki told Eve a thing or two about life and she seduced Adam with the apple, his brother Enlil became very angry, and spread the story about him being an evil snake and put a curse on Eve and all her female descendants to carry the yoke of pain and servitude for ever more.

In Mesoamerica, the Toltec Mayan god Gucumatz was described as a 'serpent of wisdom' or the 'feathered serpent' who enlightened humankind. His Aztec counterpart was named Quetzalcoatl. In Yucatan, he is called Kukulcan.

The Hopi refer to a race of reptoids called Sheti, or 'snake brothers' who live underground. And the Cherokee, and other Native American peoples, also refer to reptoid races.

In pre-Columbian mythology from Colombia, Bachue (the primordial woman) transformed into a big snake. She is also sometimes called the 'celestial snake, or 'serpiente celestial'.

In Indian scriptures and legends, the Nagas are reptilian beings said to live underground and interact with human beings on the surface. In some versions, these beings were said to have once lived on a continent in the Indian Ocean that sank beneath the waves.

The Chinese, Korean and Japanese speak throughout their history of 'L-ng' ('Yong' in Korea, 'Ryu' in Japanese) or dragons, conceived of in both physical and non-physical forms, but rarely depicted in humanoid form, though they may assume a non-reptilian human form.

In the Middle East, reptilian beings ranging from certain jin to dragons and serpent men, have been spoken of since ancient times.

In Africa, some shamans claim to bear extensive esoteric knowledge of a race of reptilians called Chitauri, whom they say control Earth. They also claim to have accounts of a reptilian race who created them and used them to work their gold mines. The Zulu shaman Credo Mutwa claims the Zulu people have known of a reptilian species for centuries. He is the official historian of the Zulu people. He mentions amphibious beings from Sirius in his book *Song of the Stars*.

In Australia, the aboriginal people have carefully preserved legends of the serpent in their so-called "Dreamtime" myths of the earth's creation.

(Source: http://www.crystalinks.com/reptilians.html)

Eventually, the Anunnaki did lose control of Earth and its population, which was rapidly expanding with mankind scattered across the globe forming their own colonies. And although the primitive tribes still followed the serpent ideology, many of the more established nations were following their own particular gods listed below:

The Names of the Gods

The Nibiruan Council of Twelve and their names are translated into the following language groups:

NIBIRUAN	ANU	ANTU	NINKHURSAG	ISHKUR
SUMERIAN	ANSHAR	APSU/NINTUD	NINMAH	ADAD
HITTITE			NINTI	TESHUB
EGYPTIAN	GEB/SEB	NUT/NEITH	ISIS	HORUS
GREEK	KRONOS	RHEA	HERA	ARES
ROMAN	SATURN	OPS	JUNO	MARS
SANSKRIT	SAVITAR	ADITI	ADITI	MITRA
HINDI	TVASHTAR	APO	HARITI	MITHRAS
MAYAN	AKANCHOB	AKNA	COATLICUE	HUITZILOPOCHTI
INCAN	INTI/PUNCHAU	QUILLA	PACHAMAMA	VIRACOCHA RIMAC
TEUTONIC	BURI/MANNUS	TUISTO	EDUN/BESTLA	TIW/TYR/VE
SLAVONIC	SVAROG	MATI-ZEMLYA	DENNITSA	PERUN
FINNO-UGRIC	UKKO	AKKA/RAUNI	MADER-AKKA	ARIANROD

Our Ancestors From the Stars

CELTIC	EOCHARD	DANU/ANU	BOANNA	ANGUS/OG
NIBIRUAN	**ENLIL**	**NINLIL**	**ENKI**	**NINKI**
SUMERIAN	ASSHUR	NAMMU	EA/URKI	DAMKINA
EGYPTIAN	OSIRIS	MA'AT	PTAH - KHNUM	NEPHTHYS
CANAANITE	BA'AL	ASHERAH		
SEMITIC	YAHWEH ALLAH EL		ADONAI	
GREEK	ZEUS	MAIA	POSEIDON HEPHAESTUS	LIBYA
ROMAN	JUPITER	MAJESTA	VULCAN	AFRICA
SANSKRIT	INDRA	INDRANI	AGNI	SVAHA
HINDI	VISHNU	MAYA	AHRIMAN/ SHIVA	GANGA
MAYAN	TLALOC	CHALCHIUTLICUE	ITZAMNA	???
INCAN	CATEQUIL/ PILAN	CUYCHA		
TEUTONIC	THOR/ DONAR	JØRD	HOENIR	???
SLAVONIC	DAZHBOG	MYESYATS	OGON	MARZANNA
INNO-UGRIC	ILMA	???	AHTI	VELLAMO
CELTIC	DAGDA	GWYDIAN	MANANNAN	???

NIBIRUAN	**NANNAR**	**ISH.KUR**	**UTU**	**INANNA**
SUMERIAN	SIN	ADAD	SHAMASH	ISHTAR
EGYPTIAN	THOTH		HARPOCRATES	HATHOR
CANAANITE		BA'AL MOLOCH		
SEMITIC	ALLAH	YAHWEH		
GREEK	HERMES		APOLLO	APHRODITE
ROMAN	MERCURY		HELIOS	VENUS
SANSKRIT	SUDHANVAN		RUDRA	USHAS
HINDI	BUDDHA		RAMA	LAKSHMI
MAYAN	QUETZALCOATL		XOCHIPILI	TLAZOLTEOTL
INCAN	PIHUECHENYL		TAMENDONARE	CHASCA
TEUTONIC	ODIN/WODEN		ULL/MAGNI	FRIJI/FRIGG
SLAVONIC	VOLGA		VARPULIS	KUPALA

NIBIRUAN	MARDUK	NINURTA	NERGAL	NINGISHZIDDA
FINNO-UGRIC	VOGUL		???	???
CELTIC	LUG/LLEW		NUADA/LUDD	BRIGIT
SUMERIAN	BEL	NINGIRSU-NIMROD	ERRA	
ASSYRIAN	ASHUR			
EGYPTIAN	RA (AMON-RA)			TEHUTI / THOTH
GREEK				HERMES
MESOAMERICA				QUETZALCOALT KUKULKAN XIUHTECUHTLI TOPILTZIN

(Source: https://www.bibliotecapleyades.net/sitchin/sitchinbooks.htm "Sumerian Table of Gods")

The present World History Timeline found in our History Books

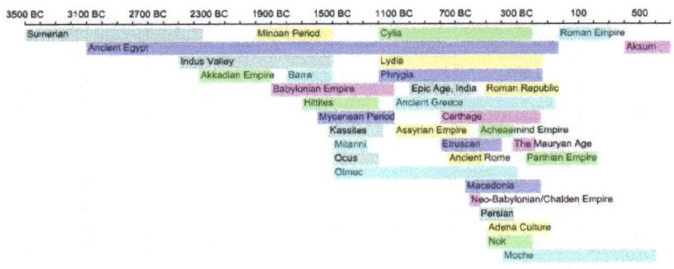

(Source: http://zdrav40.ru/?k=World+History+Timeline+Ancient+Egyptian+civilization)

The History of the Caduceus

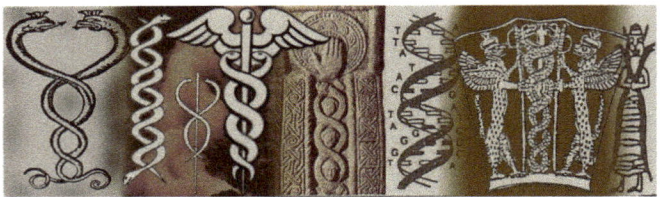

(Source: http://www.mesopotamiangods.com/ningishzidda/)

The Sumerian seal in the above picture is a depiction of the serpent god Ningiszida, dating from approximately 2000 BCE. The god itself is the two copulating snakes entwined around an axial rod. It is accompanied by two gryphons.

(Source: https://commons.wikimedia.org/wiki/File:Ningizzida.jpg)

The caduceus is one of the most ancient of symbols. You might best know this symbol as the DNA structure and healing used by the medical profession. Since ancient Mesopotamia, the caduceus presented two serpents intertwined (the central nervous system) around a staff (the spinal column) with the wings (the swan) on either side (the two hemispheres of the brain, with the circle in the centre representing the pineal gland, or the central sun and psychic centre within). It also symbolized the kundalini energy.

This was originally the symbol for the Anunnaki-Sirian creator god, EA, or EN.KI (who has become an archetype), and was the chief of the magicians, 'the one who knows', and infamous for being the serpent of the Garden of Eden who created lifeforms in test tubes half a million years ago with his half-sister Ninharsag, at the suggestion of his son, Marduk, to create humans to be the workers for the gods. (The symbol is also based upon the winged globe for the planet Nibiru, the symbol of the royal Anunnaki family.)

It is interesting to note that when the Anunnaki departed Earth, Enlil's family was given the Sinai, and Enlil's son, Sin, became its new ruler. His symbol is the crescent moon, which became the symbol for Islam.

(Source: https://www.bibliotecapleyades.net/sumer_anunnaki/ esp_sumer_anunnaki07.htm)

The caduceus was also carried by the Greek god Hermes and the Roman god Mercury, the winged messengers of the gods and patrons of commerce. (And is also the cap badge of the Royal Corps of Signals, my husband's old regiment.)

The Reason the Ancient Gods Are Depicted with Animal Heads

Writing was only invented about 6,000 years ago, and for several thousand years after writing developed, only a small group of people, scribes and priests could read and write, so the only way to convey complex ideas to people was through art and symbolism.

The gods and goddesses were real people, but in art they were shown with particular animal features. For example:

A gryphon – the amalgamation of a lion and eagle is used to denote strength and military courage (leadership/king of beasts/king of birds).

- **The head and or the body of a lion** – ferociousness.
- **Hawk** – God of the sky, protector of kings.
- **Falcon** – god of the moon.
- **Jackal** – protector of the dead.
- **Ibis or baboon** – god of scribes.

Giants

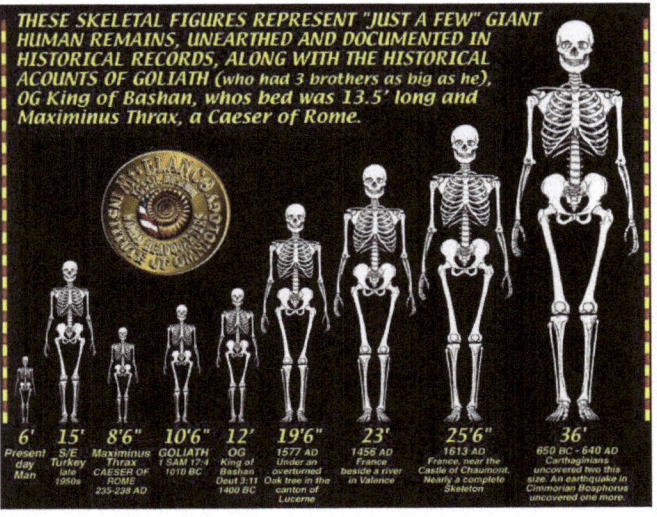

Of all the chapters I researched, this was the most difficult to unravel, because plodding through the many myths, cover-ups and the various interpretations of Genesis 6 in the Bible has at times been somewhat confusing. What follows is a very brief synopsis of my findings, so I shall start with a quote from Wikipedia:

'*According to Genesis 6:4 of the Bible, "The Nephilim were the offspring of the 'sons of God' and the 'Daughters of men' before the Deluge."*

According to Numbers 13:33, they later inhabited Canaan at the time of the Israelite conquest of Canaan.

An either similar or identical biblical Hebrew term, read as "Nephlim" by some scholars, or as the word "fallen" by others, appears in Ezekiel 32:27.

The word is loosely translated as "giants" in some Bibles and left untranslated in others. They are mentioned in the following two contexts in the Bible:

Genesis Chapter 6:1-4 (New Revised Standard Version)

"When people began to multiply on the face of the ground, and daughters were born to them, the sons of God saw that they were fair, and they took wives for themselves of all that they chose. Then the Lord said, 'My spirit shall not abide in mortals forever, for they are flesh; their days shall be one hundred twenty years.' The Nephilim were on the earth in those days – and also afterward – when the sons of God went to the daughters of humans, who bore children to them. These were the heroes that were of old, warriors of renown.'"

Thus, from the above source, the Nephilim were the 'sons' of the union between sons of God who were supposedly fallen angels according to classical Judaic explanations and the daughters of man descended from Adam.

From Wes Penre's *Shamens of MU: Fallen Angels and Corruption of Wisdom*, (http://wespenre.com/2/shamans-of-mu-fallen-angels-and-corruption-of-wisdom.htm and scroll down to '8. A Gigantic visit from the Pleiades') we find who these fallen angels were and where they originally came from.

'*While the "humans were going forth and multiplying on earth", Enki, being the genetic scientist he was, wanted to expand his creations (humans) by perhaps adding an extra set of genes to our DNA. So he went to the Pleiades, who were giants with blond to red hair and blue eyes, and brought 200 Pleiadians back to Earth to assist him with genetic experiments and help him teach mankind.*'

Here I must digress to explain the following, which is entirely my own opinion and contradicts the general idea of who the Nephilim are:

God's angels are ETs who lived in the Pleiades. The Pleiades are part of the heavenly Orion Empire. Enki is a prince of Orion. The term 'falling' means they fell (came) down from heaven, a much higher dimension, to the third dimension of matter: Earth.

It's here I find myself in a bit of a quandary, and not quite able to tie up the dates. The giants were created before the flood. The flood was orchestrated around 10,500 BC specifically to get rid of all humans, including the giants who were causing too much havoc here on Earth. The next time the giants are mentioned is in the Bible book of Numbers, which seems to be discussing events thousands of years after Noah's flood.

There is more information regarding giants in the chapter about the Anunnaki, but here we are concerned about the giants mentioned in the Bible, and the following clue comes from Numbers 13:1-2; 21, 27-28; 32-33 (New Revised Standard Version):

'*The Lord said to Moses, "Send men to spy out the land of Canaan. Which I am giving to the Israelites." [...] So, they went up and spied out the land [...] And they told him [...] "yet the people who live in the land are strong, and the town are fortified and very large; and besides, we saw the descendants of Anak there." So, they brought to the Israelites an unfavourable report of the land they had spied out, saying, "The land that we had gone through as spies is the land that devours its inhabitants; and all the people that we saw in it are of great size" [...] 'There we saw the Nephilim (the Anakites come from the Nephilim); and to ourselves we seemed like grasshoppers, and so we seemed to them."'*

The Lord in this case is Enlil (YHVH) the god of the Torah and the Old Testament.

In searching for an approximate timeline, I found that archaeologists recognise that Canaan is a general name for the land and its inhabitants during what is called 'the Middle and Late Bronze Age' (2000-1200 BC).

Next is Deuteronomy 20:16-18 (New International Version (NIV), and the order is very specific: *'You shall save alive nothing that breathes, but you shall utterly destroy them [...] as the Lord your God has commanded: that they may not teach you to do according to all their abominable practices, which they have done in the service of their gods and so to sin against the Lord your God.'*

Joshua 11:23 (KJV) says: *'So Joshua took the whole land, according to all that the Lord had said to Moses; and Joshua gave it as an inheritance to Israel.'*

The following clue comes from Mary Sutherland's *Giant Gods and Lost Races*:

'After the Canaanites were vanquished by the Israelites the refugees pushed further into Africa: "There (in Egypt) multiplying, the Canaanites pierced further into Africa; where they possessed all the land unto the 'Pillars of Hercules'." *The Canaanites built the cities of Tinge and Tanger in Numida. Here was found two pillars of white stone. Engraved on these stones at Tanger was found the inscription:* "We are those exiles that were governors of the Canaanites, but have been driven away by Joshua the thief, and have come here to live."*

From Numidia, the Canaanites soon made it across the Straits of Gibraltar and reached as far north as Scandinavia and the British Isles. In these countries (and Europe in general) they have left evidence of their existence over large areas of land, which is evident due to the numerous skeletons which have subsequently been dug up. They are known as the "Beaker People" to the anthropologists for their pottery and drinking vessels that had long been woven in North Africa out of esparto grass.'

In Mary Sutherland's book *The Red-haired Giants, Atlantis in North America (In Search of the Ancient Man Book 2)*, she shows evidence that strongly supports that races of Atlantean giants lived in North America and were the advent of the smaller races of modern men and women. As thousands of earthen burial mounds attest, constant war against one another caused their numbers to diminish and the smaller, but more numerous races, eventually subjugated them.

I conclude this chapter by quoting *The Encyclopaedia of Ancient Giants in North America* by Fritz Zimmerman, Foreword by L.A. Marzulli which '*chronicles two distinct waves of giant humans migrating to North America. As early as 7,000 BC, strange people arrived on the North American shores of gigantic size with Neanderthal-looking skulls. Their spread across landscape is documented not only by their massive skeletons, but by an identical material culture that was found buried with their remains. Double rows of teeth and skulls with protruding horns make them one of America's most intriguing mysteries.*

At the advent of the Bronze Age another migration of giant humans found their way to North America. A persistent legend exists with Native Americans of a people who came to trade and mine the copper from the Upper Great Lakes. They left an indelible mark upon the landscape of the Ohio Valley with their large burial mounds and earthworks aligned to solar, lunar and stellar events. The measurements of these works reveal that they were constructed with the knowledge of advanced mathematics.

The discovery of giant humans in North America is the result of pouring through over 10,000 state, county and township histories at one of the largest genealogical libraries in America. Hundreds of additional accounts were also found within newspaper archives. The result is the LARGEST COMPILATION of Giant Human Skeletons Discovered in America, *in print.*'

(You can find more information about giants on http://wespenre. com/2/shamans-of-mu-fallen-angels-and-corruption-of-wisdom.htm Scroll down to 7. "Proof of Giants in Ancient Times")

Ancient Underground Tunnels And Cities

Dr Heinrich Kusch, the German archaeologist, states in his book *Secrets of The Underground Door to an Ancient world,* (German Title: *Tore Zur Unterwelt*) that there are thousands of 12,000-year-old underground tunnels. He states: *'These tunnels stretch from the north of Scotland to Turkey right down to the Mediterranean. They do not all link up but taken together it is a massive underground network. Ancient mankind had the knowledge and tools to build complex structures over thousands of years ago. Evidence of that are the Pyramids of Bosnia in Europe and their underground tunnels go for kilometres.'*

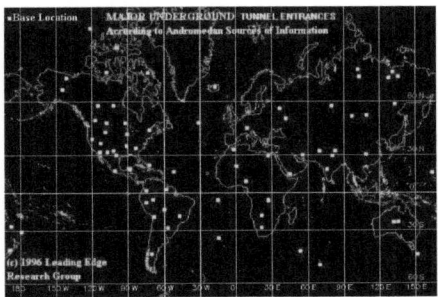

Turkey – In Cappadocia in Turkey there is the underground city of Derinkuyu. This is a multi-level underground city in the Nevsehir Province. Extending to a depth of approximately sixty metres (200 feet), it is large enough to have sheltered as many as 20,000 people together with their livestock and food stores. The city can be closed from the inside with large stone doors. Each floor can be closed off separately.

It has all the amenities found in other underground complexes across Cappadocia such as wine and oil presses, stables, cellars, storage rooms, refectories and chapels.

Between the third and fourth levels is a vertical staircase to a cruciform church on the lowest (fifth) level.

The large fifty-five-metre (180-foot) ventilation shaft appears to have been used as a well. The shaft also provided water to both the villagers above and, if the outside world was not accessible, to those in hiding. *(Source: Wikipedia)*

City of Derinkuyu in Turkey

Russia – The shaft in the ancient underground megalith at Kabardino-Balkaria in Russia is so huge it leaves one with the impression that it is a buried megalith after all, rather than something built underground. The construction of a megalith the size of those at Giza, in a manmade mountain, points towards either extraterrestrial assistance or a technologically advanced race of humanity. The engineering challenges associated with such a technical marvel could only have been successfully met by a very smart group of engineers, architects and builders.

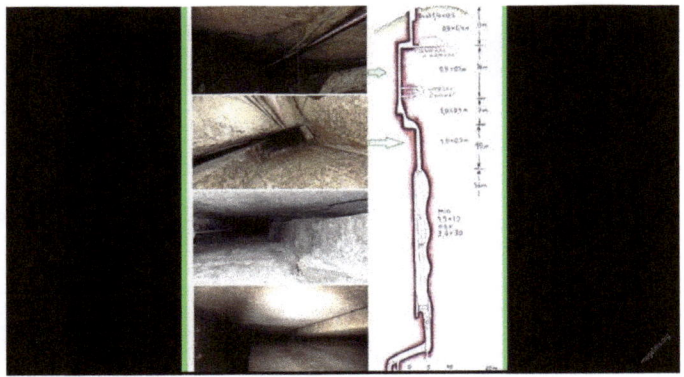

Megalith at Kabardino in Russia

Italy – In Orvieto in Italy there is a large underground city made up of approximately 1,200 caves that crisscross and overlap far underneath the urban fabric, which show identical signs of extreme age and design elements like the underground cities of Cappadocia, subsequently used and remodelled by later cultures (as everywhere else again).

Orvieto in Italy

Subterranean Tunnels and Underground Alien Bases

Evidence from around the world, indicates that the people from Atlantis and Mu were hi-tech survivors of the cataclysmic flood which destroyed their islands. And like the nuclear survival bunkers and secret research facilities of our own civilization, these were those who arose from the underground 'cities of the gods' after the water settled. They are the fabled gods of ancient Summer, Egypt, India, South America, Japan, China and the rest.

This will sound quite unbelievable, and I do wholeheartedly agree, but I felt compelled to include the following about the underground city of Telos situated beneath Mt Shasta in Northern California.

Secrets of the Subterranean Cities

Sharula Dux is a princess of the underground city of Telos. Telos is situated beneath Mt Shasta in northern California. The ancient continent of Lemuria (Mu) relocated 25,000 of its inhabitants to Telos just prior to the destruction and sinking of the continent of Mu.

Sharula has emerged from her subterranean home to bring to the surface the higher truths that have been taught and lived for thousands of years. Her story will amaze and inspire you as you discover how Telosian live his/her life from conception all the way through adulthood.

(Source: https://www.bibliotecapleyades.net/sociopolitical/esp_sociopol_underground19.htm)

Underwater Bases

As shown on the map above there are several underwater bases and I quote, with permission, from Maximillien de Lafayette's book: *1520 Things you Don't Know About UFOs, Alien's Technology, Extraterrestrials and U.S. Black Operations. Vol 2* – published 2011.

'Corridor Plasma is an underwater cold plasma tunnel temporarily (periodically) created, used and transported by intraterrestrials (the Greys) to navigate underwater.

Intraterrestrials *are aliens who live on or in the planet.*

Extraterrestrials *are those who live off the planet, such as on their motherships which orbit high above the planet, or those who sometimes visit from their own individual planets. They are able to move around the oceans by using Corridor Plasma and the Vacuum Tunnel:*

The corridor consists of a movable aquatic web of 17 underwater channels that link the aliens to their habitats, headquarters and communities.

By using these cold plasma tunnels, UFOs can accomplish extraordinary tasks, such as, to name a few:
- *To reach an astonishing speed*
- *To avoid sonar detection*
- *To remain undetected by spy satellites*
- *To enter and exit underwater bases*

One of the most amazing aspects of this technology is the fact that the aliens' underwater crafts never touch the water. There is a plasma shield surrounding the exterior body of the craft. We know that plasma produces extreme heat. And this heat can melt the craft. But the aliens found a way to isolate the plasma heat from the body of the craft, by adding two layers of anti-plasma shields (called a plasma belt) to the exterior body of the craft. The corridor plasma is moveable and mobile, meaning the aliens can place the underwater tunnels, and displace them according to their needs, and "navigate chart".

The tunnels extend to thousands of miles underwater, and serve as a web network for several alien underwater bases around the globe.'

Svalbard Global Seed Vault in Norway

Worldwide, more than 1,700 gene banks hold collections of food crops for safekeeping; yet many of these are vulnerable, exposed not only to natural catastrophes and war, but also to avoidable disasters, such as lack of funding or poor management. Something as mundane as a poorly functioning freezer can ruin an entire collection. And the loss of a crop variety is as irreversible as the extinction of a dinosaur, animal or any form of life.

It was the recognition of the vulnerability of the world's gene banks that sparked the idea of establishing a global seed vault to serve as a backup storage facility from the world's crop collections.

Permafrost and thick rock ensure that the seed samples will remain frozen, even without power. The vault is the ultimate insurance policy for the world's food supply; offering options for future generations to overcome the challenges of climate change and population growth, and it will secure, for centuries, millions of seeds representing every important crop variety available in the world today. It is the final back up.

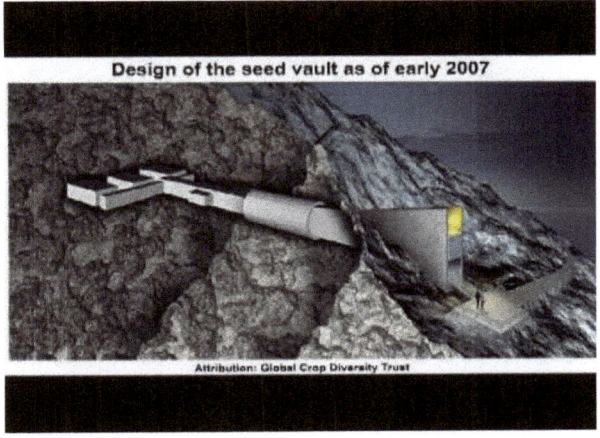

(Source: permission granted by the Global Crop Diversity Trust)

Switzerland – The world's longest and deepest twin-bore Gotthard base tunnel provides a 57km high-speed rail link under the Swiss Alps between northern and southern Europe. It took seventeen years to build, at a cost of over twelve billion Swiss francs (eleven billion Euros), with 125 labourers rotating in three shifts to lay the tunnel's slab track in 43,800 hours of non-stop work, according to the Swiss rail service. It was as opened on 1st June 2016.

The tunnel has overtaken Japan's 53.9km Seikan rail tunnel as the longest in the world, and pushed the 50.5km channel tunnel linking the UK and France into third place. Below is a picture of the giant tunnelling machine used.

Our Ancestors From the Stars

Giant tunnelling machine

June Rye

Crop Circles and Stone Circles

Crop Circles

Twenty-six countries reported approximately 10,000 crop circles in the last third of the twentieth century. Over ninety percent of them were proved to be not manmade. Circles appear overnight, although some are reported to have appeared during the day.

Governments have published several documents to convince people that crop circles are hoaxes and manmade regardless of the fact that the genuine formations are made according to the sacred or Euclidian geometry using the vital numbers 5, 6 and 7.

There are a series of peculiarities that exclude the work of pranksters. Researchers found that the molecular composition of the crops within the circle had changed, and it is unknown how the stalks can be bent at ninety-degree angles without breaking them, while different layers are pointing in different directions, sometimes even interwoven like braided hair. The plants also live on, but grow horizontally instead of vertically. Researchers have not been able to reproduce any of these phenomena successfully.

In the picture below are a few examples of different geometrical shapes pieced together to form each crop circle.

Geometrical crop circles

In 1974, the most powerful broadcast ever deliberately beamed into space was made from Puerto Rico. The broadcast formed part of the ceremonies held to mark a major upgrade to the Arecibo radio telescope. The transmission consisted of a simple pictorial message at our putative cosmic companions in the globular star cluster M-13. This cluster is roughly 25,000 light years from us, near the edge of the Milky Way galaxy, and contains approximately a third of a million stars.

The broadcast was particularly powerful because it used Arecibo's megawatt transmitter attached to its 305-metre antenna. The latter concentrates the transmitter energy by beaming it into a very small piece of sky. The emission was equivalent to a twenty trillion-watt omnidirectional broadcast, and would be detectable by a SETI (Search for Extraterrestrial Intelligence) experiment just about anywhere in the galaxy assuming a receiving antenna similar in size of Arecibo's. Initially the message was only intended as a demonstration of transmissional technology, not as a serious attempt to make contact. In fact, it's so far away that in 25,000 years, when it finally reaches its destination, its destination will have moved!

What happened next? In 2001 the following crop circle appeared in Chilbolton, England with the following message:

The message within the disc was deciphered using the standard 8-bit binary code known as ASCII (American Standard Code for Information Interchange). The cipher starts at the centre of the disk and spirals outward counter-clockwise – this is also the same read pattern that a compact disc or DVD uses – and was translated as this image:

(You can find out the full significance of the above image and the next image by following this link: http://humansarefree. com/2011/02/two-most-important-alien-messages.html)

Our Ancestors From the Stars

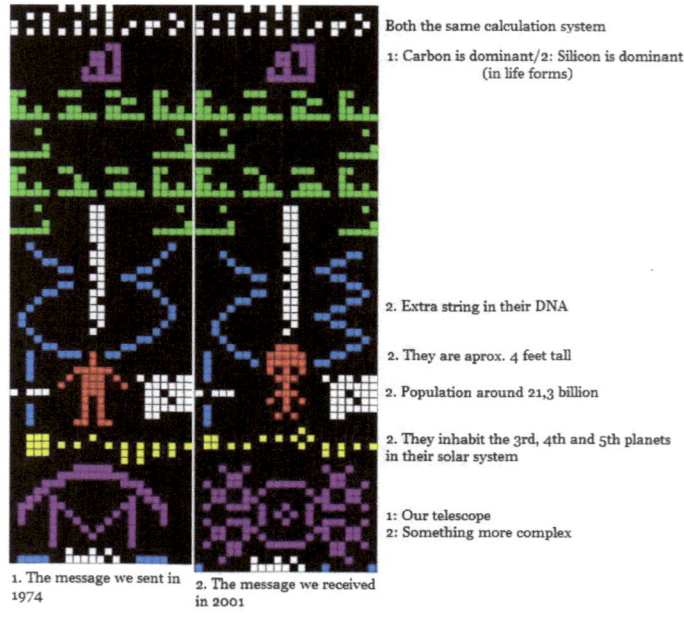

Both the same calculation system

1: Carbon is dominant/2: Silicon is dominant
(in life forms)

2. Extra string in their DNA

2. They are aprox. 4 feet tall

2. Population around 21,3 billion

2. They inhabit the 3rd, 4th and 5th planets in their solar system

1: Our telescope
2: Something more complex

1. The message we sent in 1974
2. The message we received in 2001

(Source: Dr Horace Drew – "Decoding Crop Circles"
https://www.youtube.com/watch?v=gA1gF8FtyoI)

Stone Circles

The fact that the shadow of an object changes its position on the ground in a regular way is also one of those key astronomical facts that also seems older than the written historical record. Temple and monument architecture also shows that many ancient civilizations knew how to use the changing solar shadow as a local clock to measure the daily passage of time.

Once you have a sense that the position of the sun's shadow can be measured in a practical way to mark the passage of time, it is not such a major leap to recognise that from day to day, the length of this shadow, and the sun's rising and setting each day, also change but more slowly. The passage of the seasons is easily seen in the changing circumstances of the rising and setting location of the sun along the southern horizon, and in its maximum noon-time height in the southern sky. Astronomers call this the Meridian Transit.

Almost universally, civilizations have eventually discovered the importance of the Spring Equinox as the start of the planting season. In very arid locations, such as the southwest desert of the United States, the growing season is short due to rainfall patterns, so it is important to know within days when to plant. Spring also had important religious connotations as the 'rebirth' of the world from the grip of winter – a time for both joyous festivities and solemn ceremony. Astronomically, this happens when the sun rises on the eastern horizon, halfway between its extreme winter position and its extreme summer position. By carefully noting these three locations on the horizon, you can anticipate when winter has ended and the seasons are moving towards spring. It was common for this equinoctial position to be encoded into important buildings through sightlines in the monument architecture, such as the windows that let the light from the sun reach an interior wall only at the appointed day during the year.

(Source: Technology Through Time by Dr Sten Odenwald http://sunearthday.nasa.gov/2011/articles/ttt_72.php)

Stonehenge in England

Stonehenge is positioned at the centre of a network where fourteen major ley lines converge, making it a very powerful vortex or energy portal. According to Aubrey Burl, the British archaeologist, there are 1,303 stone circles located in the UK. Many stone circles connect up with Stonehenge, but its importance is its connection with the Great Pyramid at Giza, which in turn connects it with many other ancient monuments around the world.

The local population were taught rudimentary skills of planting and harvesting and the ETs supervised and helped them to construct their own stone circles. The priests taught specific elders or chiefs how to interoperate the direction

I wrote about Stonehenge in *Aquarius*, but here is a quick recap from *English Heritage – History of Stonehenge:*

'Stonehenge is perhaps the world's most famous prehistoric monument. It was built in several stages: the first monument was an early henge monument, built about 5,000 years ago, and the unique stone circle was erected in the late Neolithic period about 2,500 BC.'

(Source: reconstruction drawing by Alan Sorrell by permission of Historic England Archive)

Dolores Cannon (1931-2014) visited Stonehenge several months before her death, and the following information comes from her book *The Search for Hidden, Sacred Knowledge – The Original Stonehenge*:

'The original structure was built around the same time as the Great Pyramid by the survivors of Atlantis after it was destroyed during the Deluge, around 10,500 BC.

Stonehenge was an observatory, and like other large ancient structures was built as an "energy beacon" aligned to particular ET's home planets or constellations, and served as markers for spaceships orbiting the planet so they could know where their brothers were located and working. It also served as a large calendar in order to calculate time, especially the passing of the seasons so that they would know when to plant and when to harvest. Special ceremonies were held to mark the times of the summer and winter solstices, and the spring and autumn equinox.'

(Source: https://www.youtube.com/watch?v=NoDjgXwkkqg: "Dolores Cannon Visits Stonehenge" permission given by Ozark Mountain Publishing Inc.)

She mentions that there was a portal in the centre of the circle of stones which used to open during particular ceremonies and one could visit other dimensions. It was a place of peace and love, until one day the Norse men invaded the site. Some of the elders managed to get away, except for one who was tortured and killed on the portal which destroyed the positive energy. It was after that that the lintel stones were taken down to destroy the negative energy. These were the ancestors of the Druids.

Southern Africa

Scattered throughout the mountains of Mpumalanga, in the north of South Africa, Michael Tellinger in *African Temples of the Anunnaki – The Lost Technologies of the Gold Mines of*

Enki has estimated that there are at least 100,000 ancient stone circles, of which most seem to be connected to an expansive network of channels that are often misinterpreted as 'roads' by some historians. This connected grid of circular ruins is in an expanse of ancient agricultural terraces surrounding the structures.

The Zimbabwean archaeologist, Roger Summers, confirms that there are thousands of ruins and terraces scattered throughout the following countries of Botswana, Zimbabwe and South Africa covering more than 500,000 square miles.

(Source: Michael Tellinger from *African Temples of the Anunnaki*)

There can be no doubt the Sumerian texts are correct in their description of ancient gold mines in Southern Africa, which go as far back as 280,000 years ago. There are literally hundreds of ancient gold mines dotted around Botswana, Zimbabwe and South Africa. South Africa is the place where most of the gold in the world has been mined in modern history. It was no different in ancient times.

June Rye

It has been estimated by the DeBeers Mining Corporation that there at least 75,000 of these ancient gold mines, and in 1992 one of the ancient shafts they found went down 23,000 feet and was cut with absolute precision, indicating advanced laser technology.

The circle below, situated in North West of South Africa, is aptly named 'Adam's Calendar', sometimes referred to as 'African Stonehenge' and predates both Stonehenge and the Great Pyramid of Giza by tens of thousands of years. The calculation by Rodney Hale shows the plan of Adam's calendar with alignments as they were in 11,500 BC. *Which is 1,000 years before the Great flood of Noah.*

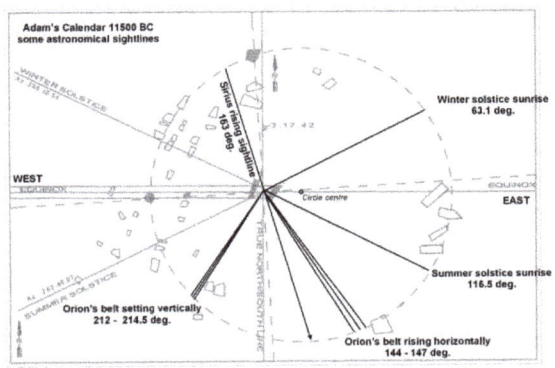

(Source: Michael Tellinger from African Temples of the Anunnaki)

I should point out that once again we are involved with Sirius, Orion and the Great Pyramid. And I am absolutely sure that the Anunnaki (descendants of the Sirius/Orion Empire) are leaving us in no doubt that they were the predominant creators of the Human Race.

Great Zimbabwe

Below we have the ruins of the Great Zimbabwe, presumably the headquarters of Enki, the serpent god described in the Sumerian tablets, as the picture below shows its exact alignment with the Great Pyramid of Giza.

This is a ruined city that was once the capital of the Kingdom of Zimbabwe, which existed from around 1,100 to 1,450. The word 'Great' distinguishes the site from many hundreds of small ruins around that part of the world. It lies approximately 500 miles from the site of Adam's Calendar. Artefacts show that the city formed part of a trade network extending as far as China. It is in this very region that one finds scattered throughout the strata and rocks deposits of reef and alluvial gold, iron, talc, asbestos and nickel, offering a reasonable explanation for such a high concentration of ancient structures.

Ann Kritzinger, a geologist from the University of Zimbabwe, has shown in several papers that many of the ruins in Zimbabwe were most likely for the purpose of extracting and purifying gold – and were not slave pits, animal pits or grain pits as is often suggested by ignorant scholars.

Dr Cyril Hromnik writes in great detail in *Indo Africa* (1981) about the Hindu Dravidians from the Makomati tribe who were in southern Africa mining gold as far back as 2,000 years ago, and probably even further back in time.

June Rye

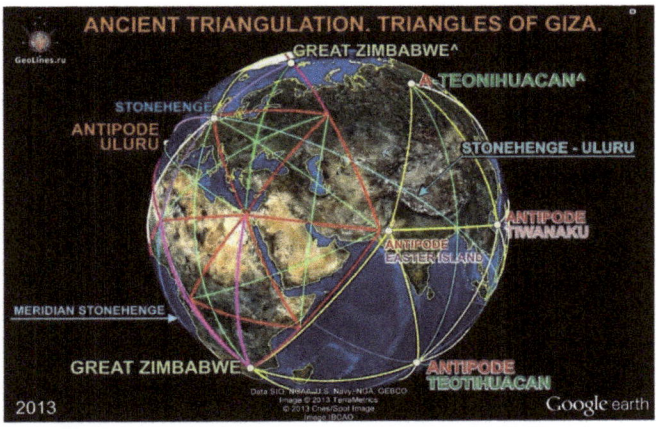

One can also see how all the predominant ancient sites are connected and aligned with each other on the Planetary Grid System

Judging from the dates, the Anunnaki were running their gold mining operation in Africa, and it is logical to assume that the deluge which happened around 10,500 BC would have completely devastated that part of Africa. Assuming there were survivors at the top of the mountains, everything else would have been overrun by the water and covered by soil and sand. That is perhaps why the majority of the stone ruins lie below the soil with the top parts barely visible.

To Sum Up

- We know from the Sumerian tablets that Enki (the serpent god) was in charge of the southern half of Africa. And presumably his headquarters was Great Zimbabwe.
- Great Zimbabwe was aligned with the Great Pyramid at Giza: his contact with his Orion/Sirius/Draco family.
- Although we can assume that all the dwellings were destroyed in the deluge, what happened to the people? It is obvious there were thousands of people working

and living in that part of the world. But the greatest mystery of all is: what happened to them? Why have their remains never been found? It would seem they just completely vanished from the radar!

(Source: Great Zimbabwe National Monument (Zimbabwe) © Graciela Gonzalez Brigas)

Megaliths

A megalith is a large stone that has been used to construct a structure or monument, either alone or together with other stones. The word 'megalithic' describes structures made of such large stones without the use of mortar or concrete, representing periods of prehistory characterised by such constructions.

The ancient civilisations built megalithic stone structures along ley lines and at the intersecting nodal points. Some were aligned to the solstice points on the horizon (points where the sun rises or sets on the summer or winter solstice), or to where the moon sets on a special day that might have been used for astronomical purposes. Later civilizations built temples, stone circles, medicine wheels and ceremonial structures on the same sites.

This was discussed in Aquarius, but here are some other examples:

Mount Shoria in Southern Siberia

On Mount Shoria in Southern Siberia there is an absolutely massive wall of granite stones, some of which are estimated to weigh more than 3,000 tons, and as you will see below, have obviously been cut with flat surfaces, right angles and sharp corners. Nothing of this scale has ever been discovered before. Its weight by far out strips The Pregnant Woman Stone of Baalbek, Lebanon which was previously thought to be the largest weighing in at approximately 1,260 ton.

So how did someone cut 3,000-ton granite stones with extreme precision, transport them up the side of a mountain and stack them forty metres high? According to the commonly accepted version of history, it would be impossible for ancient humans with very limited technology to accomplish such a thing.

Mount Shoria in Southern Siberia

Yonaguni Island in Japan

In 1987, a group of strange formations was found underwater off the coast of Yonaguni Island, Japan. These formations feature flat parallel edges, right angles, sharp edges, pillars and columns, leading many to believe that the site could be manmade. The last time this area would have been dry land was eight to ten thousand years ago, during the most recent ice age, and so if Yonaguni really was constructed by humans, it would be one of the oldest structures on Earth, and would drastically change what we think we know of prehistory.

Yonaguni Island in Japan

Easter Island

Little is known about the giant stone statues on Easter Island. Over 880 statues, called moai, can be found on this isolated island, which is one of the most remote inhabited islands on Earth. It was first thought that the statues were merely heads, but excavation has shown that almost all of them have bodies. Many were left in quarries, or abandoned during transport. The seven moai at Ahu Akivi face the point at which the sun sets during the equinox.

There is a form of hieroglyphic writing on some of the statues, which nobody has been able to translate. The people of Easter Island themselves are something of a mystery, too, and it remains unclear where they originally came from. One of the theories about Easter Island is that the island is actually the peak of an underwater mountain, and all that remains of the lost civilization of Mu.

Easter Island

Another example of a little clue left by our ancient ancestors for us to find, perhaps?

*(For further information: read Brien Foerster's **Rapa Nui (Easter Island):** https://www.youtube.com/watch?v=tXTrZykTjkg.)*

Kailasa Temple in Western India

This temple was carved out of a single rock block. It is one of the largest monolithic structures in the world. It is estimated that about 400,000 tons of rocks were scooped out to build this amazing structure. Most archaeologists believe that the

Kailasa Temple was completed in the eighth century, but there are others who are of the opinion it was made in 300 BC.

In my opinion, it was possibly built in the same way I 'saw' the front of the Treasury building in PETRA, Jordan, being built, and I quote from *Aquarius*: '*A picture of the front of the building was projected or printed on the front of a bare stonewall. A person in what seemed to be in a small craft, with a laser type instrument carefully proceeded to carve out the image in what seemed to be minutes. Strangely I saw no dust or bits of rock flying off the columns as they were being carved.*'

Here is a quote from *Der Spiegel* from April 1972: '*The scientists of the U.S. Laboratory for Atomic Research at Los Alamos spent a year and a half developing a thermal drill. It has nothing in common with ordinary drills. The tip of the drill is made of wolfram and heated by a graphite heating element. There is no longer any waste material from the hole being drilled. The thermal drill melts the rock through which it bores and presses it against the walls, where it cools down,*'

Perhaps this is the sort of technology that was used for carving these monuments?

Kailasa Temple at the Ellora Caves in Western India

Gobekli Tepe in Turkey

Gobekli Tepe is generally considered to be the oldest religious structure ever found. Radiocarbon dating puts the site at between 10,000 and 9,000 BC. The site contains stone structures and stone pillars which feature carvings of various predatory animals. The stone pillars – some of them reaching nearly twenty tons in weight – date to a time when humans were thought to be simple hunters-gathers.

How were these structures built at a time when humans were basically thought to have been cavemen? How did they quarry huge pieces of stone, and cut them to size with no metal tools? What was the purpose of such a site? Why did the ancient builders completely cover the whole site with soil which over centuries created a hilltop? Was this perhaps another little puzzle left by our ancestors from the stars to flame our curiosity?

Gobekli Tepe in Turkey
(Source: permission granted by Alistair Coombs)

Angkor Wat in Cambodia

There are two great complexes of ancient temples in Southeast Asia, one at Bagan in Burma, the other at Angkor in Cambodia.

The temples of Angkor, built by the Khmer civilization between 802 and 1220 AD, represent one of humankind's most astonishing and enduring architectural achievements. From Angkor, the Khmer kings ruled over a vast domain that reached from Vietnam to China to the Bay of Bengal. The structures one sees at Angkor today, more than 100 stone temples in all, are the surviving remains of a grand religious, social and administrative metropolis whose other buildings – palaces, public buildings, and houses – were built of wood and have long since decayed and disappeared.

(Source: https://sacredsites.com/asia/cambodia/angkor_wat.html)
(Source: http://whc.unesco.org/en/list/668)

Angkor Wat in Cambodia
(Source: © Vincent Ko Hon Chiu)

Angkor, in Cambodia's northern province of Siem Reap, is one of the most important archaeological sites of Southeast Asia. It extends over approximately 400 square kilometres and consists of scores of temples, hydraulic structures (basins, dykes, reservoirs, canals) as well as communication routes. For several centuries, Angkor was the centre of the Khmer kingdom. With impressive monuments, several different ancient urban plans and large water reservoirs, the site is a unique concentration of features testifying to an exceptional civilization. The architecture and layout of the successive capitals bear witness to a high level of social order and ranking within the Khmer Empire. Angkor is therefore a major site exemplifying cultural, religious and symbolic values, as well as containing high architectural, archaeological and artistic significance.

(Source: UNESCO - World Heritage Centre. Description is available under license CC-BY-SA IGO 3.0)

Ta Prohm in Cambodia

Ta Prohm in Cambodia
(Source: Claude Jaques
http://www.bible.ca/tracks/tracks-cambodia.htm)

These awesome temples were rediscovered by Portuguese adventurers and Catholic missionaries in the sixteenth century, and many were restored in the nineteenth and twentieth centuries.

Ta Prohm, one of the most picturesque, was left in its natural state. It recently gained international attention as the setting for the first Laura Croft movie.

Ta Prohm abounds with stone statues and reliefs. Almost every square inch of the grey sandstone is covered with ornate carvings. Hundreds of decorative stone circles surround familiar animals, such as monkeys, deer, water buffalo and parrots. One of the animals enclosed in the circle below is a stegosaurus.

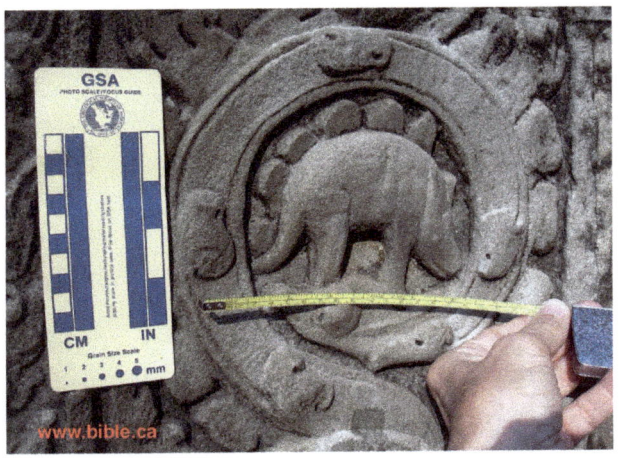

Ta Prohm: Stegosaurus surrounded by a reptile

It is abundantly clear to me that this is another clue left by our ancestors thousands of years ago for us to find at this present time.

Further Examples of Megalithic Structures

Below are examples of a few of the megalithic structures which have been found all over the world.

*(Learn more about individual sites on **The Lost History of Man** at http://talc.site88.net/mega.php "Archaeological Sites and Megalithic Structures".)*

June Rye

Pyramids and Earth's Energy Grid

Earth's energy grid is an ancient matrix of lines of subtle forces that form a pattern around the globe. These lines are known a ley lines. A ley line is a straight fault line in the earth's tectonic plates, and this is a scientific fact. What science refuses to believe, however, is that through these cracks in the earth's tectonic plates the magnetic energy released is very powerful indeed. It is therefore quite clear that the ancient civilisations who colonised this planet knew about this and that is the reason why all the ancient megalithic structures are built in specific places all over the globe: they were placed to mark and amplify and utilize the energy of particular ley line.

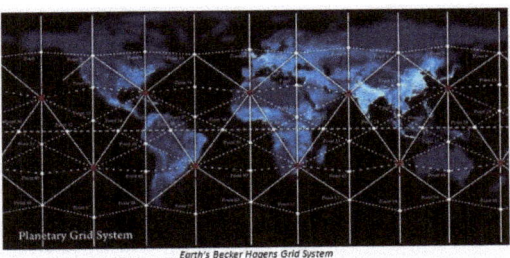

Earth's Becker Hagens Grid System

That the Great Pyramid was built exactly on the centre of the landmass of the planet, indicates to me it was put there to give us a clue of our origins by once again being aligned to the same constellation as it was all those thousands of years ago, and this time to Polaris the present pole star in the constellation of Draco. (This has already been covered in a previous chapter in *Aquarius*). I am now continuing this discussion by bringing in the mystery of the Sphinx.

I feel it is fitting to mention here that in 1968 Erich von Daniken caused a great kerfuffle when he published *Chariots of the Gods – Was God an Astronaut?* He was greatly belittled and called a charlatan, but as we know now, some of the issues he wrote about have since been proved to be true.

The official dating of the Great Pyramid of Giza is 2560 BC and for the Great Sphinx of Giza is 2500 BC, but there is now irrefutable scientific evidence that a global cataclysm did unfold between 12,800 and 11,600 years ago (10,800 – 9,600 BC), and many scientists now agree that this particular deluge was caused by a very large comet hitting the North American ice caps at the end of the last ice age. This research is well documented in Graham Hancock's *Magicians of the Gods*, published in 2015. This particular deluge takes us to the time of Noah's flood, as described in the Bible. As we've discussed, the story of a great flood or deluge is present in our culture and common across a wide range of cultures all over the world. This was also the time described by the Edgar Cayce (in *The Sleeping Prophet*) to be the time of the final sinking of Atlantis.

In the early 1990s, John Anthony West delivered a seismic shock to archaeology when he and the Boston University geologist Dr Robert Schoch revealed that the Sphinx showed evidence of rainfall erosion. Such erosion indicated in the pictures below could only mean (in my opinion) that the Sphinx was carved thousands of years before the alleged 'official' time of its completion.

The picture below shows the extent of the water erosion on the walls surrounding the Sphinx. Compare this with the picture of the Great Pyramid that shows part of its original casting stone, of which only a few survive today. Is it perhaps possible that one could have been carved before the great deluge and the other afterwards?

Erosion on the Sphinx

Original casing stones covered the whole of the Great Pyramid of Giza

We then had *The Orion Mystery – Unlocking the Secrets of the Pyramids 1994* by Robert Bauval and Adrian Gilbert. While stargazing one night, Robert Bauval, an amateur Egyptologist and engineer, at work in Saudi Arabia on an engineering project, the inspiration came to him that the layout of the three Giza pyramids on the ground beside the Nile River duplicated the layout in the sky of the three Orion Belt stars and the Milky Way. This formed the foundation of proving that the four shafts in the Great Pyramid targeted the pole stars to the north and the Orion Stars to the south, as the sky would have looked in 2500 BC. This was done by using computer simulation of the precession of the constellations that is caused by the earth's axis wobbling on a 26,000-year cycle. Another incredible revelation is that the layout of the three pyramids on the ground relative to the Nile duplicates the layout of the Orion Belt stars as it would have looked in 10,450 BC.

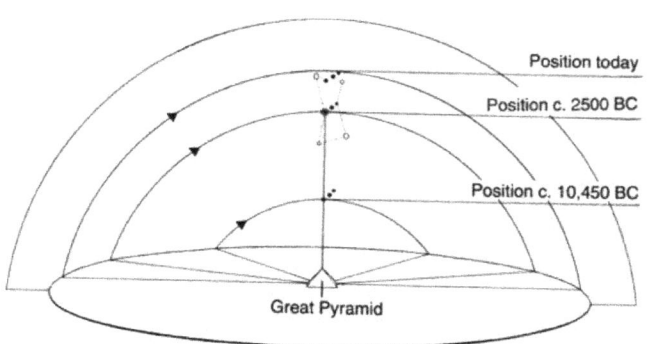

The positions of rising and culmination of Orion through the ages

Another very interesting fact is that in the picture below he had made the connection between the shafts of the king and queen's chambers both pointing in the direction of the Orion and Sirius constellations, as well as the Draco constellation.

(*Source: http://www.ancientegyptonline.co.uk/pyramid-air-shafts.html*)

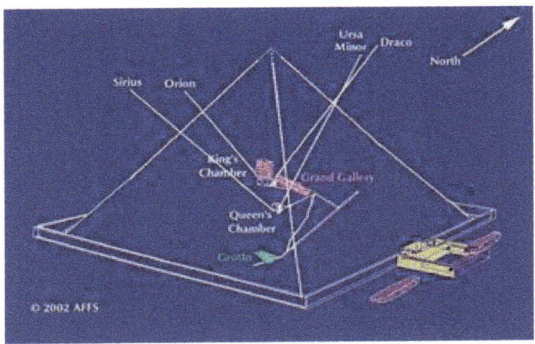

The constellation of Ursa Minor was only introduced in 600 BC. The ancient Egyptians considered Ursa Major and Minor to be part of Draco (known to the ancient Egyptians as 'the Hippo'). Draco was associated with the goddess Tawret (who took the form of a hippo).

The next clue comes from *Keepers of Genesis* (1996) by Robert Bauval and Graham Hancock. They make the connection between the Sphinx and the constellation Leo, saying: '*It is the simple fact of precession that one must go back to the "Age of Leo" beginning at around 10,500 BC, in order to obtain the "correct" sky-ground symbolism. This, as it turns out, is the only epoch in which the due-east-facing Sphinx would have manifested exactly the right symbolic alignment on exactly the right day – watching the vernal sun rising in the dawn sky against the background of his own celestial counterpart.*'

This was followed by *Heavens Mirror* (1998) by Graham Hancock. This is what he writes about the connection between Giza and Angkor: '*. . .these sites are separated by 8,000 kilometres and almost 4,000 years. More important by far, however, is the fact that both sites feature enormous monuments modelling a particular group of four constellations – Leo, Orion, Draco and Aquarius – at dawn on the spring equinox in 10,500 BC.*

At dawn on the spring equinox in 10,500 BC, Aquarius was setting due west, Leo was rising due east, Orion lay on the meridian due south, and Draco lay on the meridian due north.

> *That we have two of those constellations modelled at Giza (Leo and Orion) and the third (Draco) at Angkor seems most unlikely to be a coincidence, particularly since each one of them is oriented to a different cardinal direction. It seems obvious that careful planning must lie behind so subtle and so extenuated a scheme – and planning is the handiwork of an organization.'*

According to the picture below, not only are the pyramids of Giza associated with Orion's Belt but so are the Xian Pyramid in China and the Teotihuacan Pyramid in Mexico.

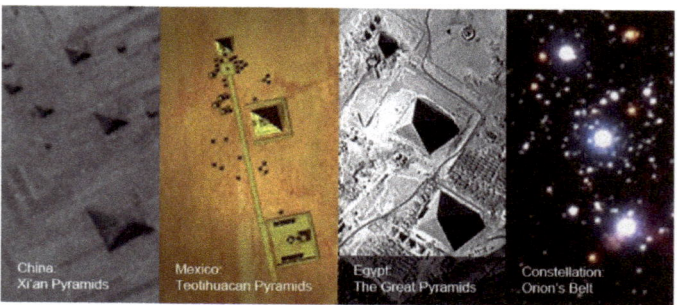

According to Alex Collier (*The Andromedan Compendium*) the Great Pyramid is part of a protective solar system grid, linking the moon and Mars monuments together to produce a force field to repel invaders. The Great Pyramid is also connected to other points on Earth such as Stonehenge, Tiahuananaco, Ayers Rock, the White Pyramid in Western China and Great Zimbabwe in Southern Africa. Together they form an energy containment field similar to an electric fence. The HAARP project (High Frequency Active Auroral Research Project) in Alaska taps into this.

Why Were the Pyramids Built?

The following comes from *Earth: An Alien Enterprise* (2013) by Timothy Good:

'Carl Anderson, an abductee whose particular alien contact had said they had originally come from Mars, and explained Earth had been colonized thousand years ago by various extraterrestrial races, and these races had been responsible for building the various pyramids.

"Primarily, the pyramids were constructed for means of generating a huge amount of energy which was used to charge their crafts when they came here from outer space," he explained in his 1966 lecture. "The cosmic energy rays of the universe came down upon the pyramids (and) these rays, upon striking the sides of the pyramids – the sides being constructed at the perfect angle – were radiated off the apex and shot for many, many hundreds of miles out into space, just like a beam from a huge searchlight, only in this case being an invisible beam. And their craft would hover over this beam and re-charge their units."

This was the reason why pyramids are built all around the earth – you can follow a circle around the earth. They're in China, they're in South America, they're in various places, constructed for the purpose of charging their units when they came here, and their energy was getting to such a low ebb that they needed charging when they had to go back again.

It's also been noted that many of these craft have been seen hovering over mountains – and the Rocky Mountains in particular – places where it is known that there are large deposits of quartz, or granite containing quartz crystals. And quartz crystals are a source that never dissipates; it's like a battery that will never run out. And so, when the energy source is harnessed from these millions of quartz crystals contained in a mountain, and especially a mountain whose peak is shaped more or less like a pyramid, so that this energy will radiate off the apex of the peak of the mountain, then they can do pretty much the same by charging as unit as they used to do from the great power pyramids.'

Our Ancestors From the Stars

Some of the pyramids found around our planet

The Alien Species Involved in Planet Earth's Evolution

Let us return now to alien involvement in Earth's evolution, and then discuss their more recent activity. It is necessary to explain here that all the extraterrestrial beings have evolved over millions of years and are so far advanced that they are able to detach their 'beings' from the physical body and return to their etheric bodies whenever they wish. Except for the Greys, they look just like us, and by allowing us to see them with a human body and a strange face is to show us what species they originally evolved from; in other words, they can easily move from one dimension to another.

According to Alex Collier (channelled by the Andromedas), due to the thousands of skirmishes over millions of years, our human DNA contains a smidgen of 'star dust' from the genes of each of the following twenty-two extraterrestrial species below:

Our Ancestors From the Stars

E.T. Races	Sentient Being Body Types	Inhabited Star Systems
Alderbaran	Human / Reptilian	Small cluster of solar systems that orbit around the star Alderbaran
Andromeda	Human	Many star systems that orbit Almach and Mirach Central Suns
Antarians	Human	Solar systems lie in a binary star System that orbits the star
Arcturians	Human / Reptilian	Smaller star systems around Bootes
Canes Venatici	Reptilian (Benevolent)	Triple Sun system; no name
Capellians	Reptilian (Neutral Now)	Three star solar systems held by gravity of the Central Star Capella
Cassiopeians	Insectual / Aquatic	Caph, Ruchbah, smaller stars; 19 solar systems
Ciakar	Reptilian	Alpha Draconis smaller star solar system Thuban-(Anwar) Giansar, Grumium, Eltanin
Cygnus Alpha	Human / Aquatic / Bird	Smaller star solar systems which orbit around the Central Suns: Deneb, Sadr, Gienah, Albireo
Hyades	Human	Binary star solar system near Alderbaran
Mintakains	Human / Aquatic	Orion- small stars around Central Sun
Mizarians	Human	Large star solar systems located between Alcor and Mizor
Nibiruan (Anunnaki)	Human / Reptilian	Bootes (Tarshem)
Orion	Human / Reptilian	Small star systems that orbit Alnilam; stars named: Syclopesus, Rigel, Betelgeuse
Pictorians	Animal / Human / Yeti (Sasquatch)	Double Star System near Kapteyn's Star
Pleiadians	Human	Small star solar systems which orbit Taygeta, Maia, Merope, Pleione, Alcyone
Procyons	Human	Single and binary star solar Systems- rich in mineral deposits
Reticulans (Zeta)	Reptilian / Plant	Small star solar systems that orbit between that stars Achernar and Canopus
Sagittaria	Human / Feline	Very large star systems between Nunki, Ascella, Media, and Kaus Australis
Sirians	Human / Reptilian / Aquatic	Muliphen, Murzim (small sister star) stars between Wezen and Aludra
Tau Cetians	Human	Star solar system that orbits between Menkar and Mira
Vega / Lyrans	Human	Small star systems which orbit Sulafat, Albireo

(Source: Alex Collier https://www.bibliotecapleyades.net/andromeda/esp_andromedacom_61.htm)

Below are a few examples of what some of the above species look like:

(Further information about the various alien species can be found on the following websites:
http://www.exopaedia.org/Extraterrestrial+Civilizations
https://www.bibliotecapleyades.net/vida_alien/esp_vida_alien_19a.htm
Barbara Lamb Presents Unique Encounters with Extraterrestrial Beings https://www.youtube.com/watch?v=b93pXHH8FzM)

Alien Abductions

There are tens of thousands of documented cases of alien contact and abductions and, in reality, probably many more we don't know about since some people either don't recall the incident (a self-imposed memory suppression as a psychological defence mechanism to protect against trauma), or are too afraid to go public with it for fear of ridicule, ostracism, or other reasons.

The pioneers of this alien abduction phenomenon were the late Harvard Professor John Mack, Professor David Jacobs, the late Budd Hopkins, John Carpenter, Yvonne Smith, the late Dolores Cannon and, more recently, Mary Rodwell and Barbara Lamb. Their résumés can be found at http://www.exopaedia.org/alpha.php.

This experience either begins when the person is at home in bed at night, or when they are in a car or out of doors. There is a buzzing sound and they are usually surrounded by a bright blue or white light. A craft with flashing lights will be hovering above, and the person is then lifted or 'floated' up into the craft. The aliens' purpose seems to vary between warnings of impending ecological catastrophes, or subjecting the person to the removal of sperm or eggs to produce half-alien half-human creatures. They are told the reason for this is because their species are on the verge of extinction, and they need human tissue and DNA to infuse with their own in order for their species to survive.

In most cases the abductors seem to be the small Greys, who are about three to four feet tall; but quite often they are accompanied by taller Greys who are about seven to eight feet tall. However, the Greys do not have a monopoly on the abductions. The abductees also describe other types as 'Lizzies' who are akin to reptiles. These come from the Draco, Ursa Major and Orion constellations.

There is also the belief that the US Government had a secret agreement with the Greys. This is according to the alleged agreement President Eisenhower made at Edwards Air Force base on 20th February 1954, allowing the Greys to abduct people on condition they would not be harmed, that they would be returned, and that they would not remember the incident. In exchange, the US Government would get highly evolved technology. Other sources mention an agreement made in 1964.

(Source: www.exopaedia.org/abductions)

Elizabeth Klarer

Elizabeth was a UFO contactee and space traveller, and this chapter would not be complete without the amazing love story of this South African woman and Akon, an astrophysicist from Menton, a planet of Proxima Centuri that, at a distance of about 4.3 light years, is our nearest stellar neighbour. Elizabeth was taken in his spaceship to Menton, where she lived with him and his family for four months and where she gave birth to their son Ayling. Akon brought Elizabeth back to Earth after the birth of their son, and continued to visit her thereafter.

Elizabeth Klarer (nee Wollatt) was born in 1910 in Mooi River, Natal, South Africa, where she grew up on a farm. She was trained as a meteorologist at Cambridge, England. She later went to Trinity College, London, to study music, where she obtained a degree. She was also a pilot and learned to fly the DeHaviland plane. During WWII, she was employed by the South African Air Force Intelligence, and during operations did work for the Royal Air Force decoding German communications. She was also trained to observe UFOs for the South African Air Force's UFO Division.

Particular interest was shown in Elizabeth's experiences by the British Ministry of Defence when they announced that UFOs do exist and are now official.

In 1975, she, as guest of honour, was given a standing ovation at the 11th International Congress for UFO Research in Germany.

In 1983, she addressed the House of Lords in England, and her paper was read at the United Nations.

In her autobiography, she explains in detail how the spaceship's light-propulsion system operates, thus allowing Akon and his people to travel across vast interstellar distances. Elizabeth died in 1994.

*(Source: **Beyond the Light Barrier** by Elizabeth Klarer – 2009)*
http://www.exopoliticssouthafrica.org/news/interviews/113-interview-with-elizabeth-klarer)

Disclosure

From the very beginning, the main reason behind the whole UFO cover-up, despite many first-hand accounts of sightings, was that society wasn't ready yet for the knowledge about alien life. So, on the one hand, programmes were set up to hide all UFO information, while at the same time other programmes were set up to start preparing society for the ultimate moment of 'disclosure'; i.e. the moment that the truth about the presence of aliens on Earth shall be revealed.

(Source: http://www.exopaedia.org/Disclosure)

Disinformation

Disinformation has long been a proven strategy of the counterintelligence community. And it has been successfully used in the UFO cover-up for decades till now, not only to be able to deny certain events, but also to discredit witnesses and researchers.

A key method in disinformation strategies is 'plausible deniability': provide information that makes a denial more credible.

(Source: http://www.exopaedia.org/Disinformation)

Press Conference Overview

Moving now, crucially, into the twenty first century, on Wednesday May 9th, 2001, over twenty military intelligence, government, corporate and scientific witnesses came forward at the National Press Club in Washington DC to establish the reality of UFOs or extraterrestrial vehicles, extraterrestrial life forms, and resulting advanced energy and propulsion technologies. The weight of their first-hand testimony, along with supporting government documentation and other evidence, will establish without any doubt the reality of these phenomena. The following is an extract from that meeting:

Don Phillips

A CIA Disclosure Project witness (one of the 2001 National Press Club witnesses that testified):
'We have records from 1954 that were meetings between our own leaders of this country and ETs here in California. And, as I understand it from the written documentation, we were asked if we would allow them to be here and do research. I have read that our reply was "Well, how can we stop you? You are so advanced." And I will say by this camera and this sound, that it was President Eisenhower that had this meeting.'

Colonel Philip Corso

A highly-decorated officer that served in Eisenhower's National Security Council in regard to the Grenada Treaty with the Zeta Reticulum Greys:
'These creatures weren't benevolent alien beings who had come to enlighten human beings. They were genetically altered human automatons, cloned biological entities actually, who were harvesting biological specimens on Earth for their own experimentation. As long

as we were incapable of defending ourselves, we had to allow them to intrude as they wished . . . We had negotiated a kind of surrender with them as long as we couldn't fight them . . . They dictated the terms because they knew what we most feared was disclosure.'

In July 1947, a UFO crashed on a ranch north west of Roswell, New Mexico, USA. The official story put out that it was a weather balloon which had crashed. In 1998, Philip Corso revealed in his book *The Day After Roswell,* the true story of the crash and what subsequently happened to the UFO and its occupants, and that it was alien technology found in that UFO that helped America develop lasers, accelerated particle-beam weapons, and aircraft equipped with 'stealth' features.

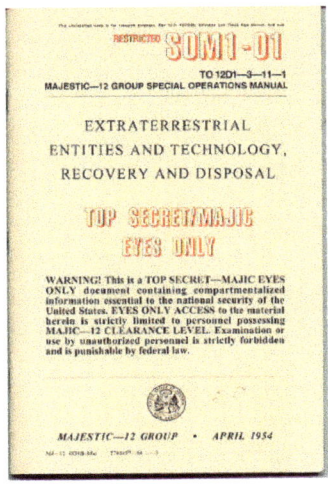

MJ-12 Special Operations Manual

(Source: http://thewebmatrix.net/disclosure/1954.html)

Major-General Wilfred de Brouwer

The following is a briefing at the National Press Club in Washington DC on 14th November 2007 by Wilfried De

Brouwer, a retired major-general of the Belgian Air Force who was chief of operations in the air staff when the Belgian UFO Wave hit. His testimony was part of the National Press Conference where pilots of different nationalities all gave testimonies of their personal experiences with UFOs (while piloting aircraft):

'My name is Wilfried de Brouwer. I am a retired Major General of the Belgian Air Force and I was Chief Operations in the Air Staff when an exceptional UFO wave took place over Belgium, indeed, during the evening of 29 November 1989 in Eastern Belgium, 140 UFO sightings were reported. Hundreds of people saw a majestic triangular craft with a span of approximately 120 feet, powerful beaming spot lights, moving very slowly without making any significant noise but, in several cases, accelerating to very high speeds.

The following days and months, many more sightings would follow. The UFO wave would last more than one year, during which a Belgian UFO organization conducted more than 650 investigations and recorded more than 400 hours of audio witness reports. On one occasion, a photograph revealed the triangular shape and four light beams of the object.

In my function of Chief Operations, I was confronted with numerous questions about the origin and nature of these craft, in the first instance, and in consultation with other NATO partners, I could confirm that no flights of stealth aircraft or any other experimental aircraft took place in the airspace of Belgium. In addition, Civil Aviation Authorities confirmed that no flight plans had been introduced and the object(s) committed infractions against the existing aviation rules.

The Belgian Air Force tried to identify the alleged intruder(s) and, on three occasions, launched F16 aircraft. On one occasion, two F16 registered rapid changes in speed and altitude which were well outside of the performance envelope of existing aircraft, in short, the Belgian UFO wave was exceptional and the Air Force could not identify the nature, origin and intentions of the phenomena.'

*(Source: UFO Blog: General Wilfried de Bouwer – **Belgium Black Triangle UFO)***

Timothy Good

A leading authority on UFOs and the alien presence – the most highly classified subject on Earth – he has written eight bestselling books since 1987. In his latest book, *Earth: An Alien Enterprise, (2013)* he mentions a conversation he had with a former member of MI6 who revealed her conversation with Neil Armstrong at a NASA conference, when he confirmed that there were 'other' spacecraft on the moon when Apollo 11 landed in 1969. He also confirmed that in subsequent Apollo missions they were often followed by UFOs and that there was an official NASA Apollo 12 photograph (AS12-497319) which clearly shows a large UFO hovering over an astronaut walking on the moon. Armstrong also confirmed that the CIA was behind the cover-up.

On the 4th August 2010, eighteen files in total were released as part of a three-year project between the National Archives and the UK Ministry of Defence. These files are made up of more than 5,000 pages of UFO reports, letters and drawings drawn from correspondence with the public and questions raised in parliament.

In June 2013, the final batch of UFO files was released by the National Archives covering the final two years of the Ministry of Defence UFO Desk (from late 2007 until November 2009).

Larry Holcombe

He writes in *The Presidents and UFO's* (2015):

'Late in the Second World War Dwight D. Eisenhower met with Winston Churchill to discuss an RAF reconnaissance aircraft encounter with a UFO near the English coastline. Churchill reportedly told Eisenhower: "This event should immediately be classified as it would create mass panic amongst the general population and destroy one's belief in the Church."'

(Source: from National Archives/UK Ministry of Defence documents released 4th August 2010 www.nationalarchives.gov. uk/documents/ufo-highlights-guide-2013.pdf will help navigate your way through the files)

Paul Hellyer

In a speech at an Exopolitic.org at the 22nd September 2014 conference, author and former Canadian Defence Minister Paul Hellyer said he believes the USA is using alien technology and feels the opportunity has been wasted:

'*We have a problem when official US policy says UFOs don't exist [...] The veil of secrecy has to be lifted now before it is too late [...] How much has been accomplished in 60 years of feverish activity by some of the most educated minds in the United States? Has America developed flying saucers that are visually indistinguishable from the Visitors as alleged, and if so what do they propose to do with them? Well, who has the answers? Well, somebody does! But, apparently, they aren't telling the Secretaries of Defence or Presidents because they don't have a "need to know".'*

Dr Michael E. Salla, MA, PhD

Author of *Galactic Diplomacy: Getting to Yes with ET"* (2013). This book introduces first-hand witness and whistle-blower testimonies revealing that the USA, Britain, Russia and other major national governments have been secretly conducting, or have known about, diplomatic relations with different extraterrestrial civilizations since at least 1952.

The following is a quote from the above book (Kindle location 3406-3413. Exopolitics Institute. Kindle Edition):

'*Chapter 6*
Extraterrestrials Among Us: Introduction
On December 7, 2012, the current Russian Prime Minister

and former President, Dmitry Medvedev, made some startling off-air comments to reporters while his microphone was still switched on. He was asked whether the President is given any secret files on extraterrestrials while in office. In his responses, Medvedev not only confided that extraterrestrials are visiting the Earth, but that some are actually living among us. [373] There is startling evidence from a number of independent sources supporting Medvedev's claim that "human-looking" extraterrestrial visitors have integrated with and lived in major population centers up until recently.

This is known by a select number of government agencies and military departments. A range of highly classified government documents and military programs give credence to this phenomenon, as revealed by a number of whistle-blowers.'

(Source: by permission from Dr Salla)

UFO Sightings by NASA Astronauts

Much evidence has been documented by former NASA astronauts, whose observations and conclusions left them in no doubt that UFOs travel around and observe Earth. Most compelling are Armstrong and Aldrin's accounts of alien craft on the moon 'warning' them to stay away; but when this was relayed back to NASA, the order was 'complete silence'.

The accounts of Major Gordon Cooper and Robert White, both Mercury astronauts in the 1960s, again offer first-hand conformation of alien craft in our skies. Many others speak of the speed and agility of the craft, far superior to theirs, and they knew they were being observed.

Maurice Chatelain, former chief of NASA Communications Systems revealed cover-ups both by NASA and the CIA, in order to 'avoid panic' amongst civilians.

Their accounts can be found at www.syti.net/UFOSightings.html. It is interesting that the accompanying video has been removed from the site.

The New UFO Documentary the Elite Hoped Would Never Be Aired in Public https://www.youtube.com/watch?v=hUr_TF9o7sY

Illuminati

The Oxford Dictionary defines 'illuminati' as 'persons enlightened spiritually or intellectually'. In modern times, the term 'illuminati' refers to a conspiratorial organisation that is said to mastermind current world affairs. These organisations control the secret societies, secret service, banking and money, politics, intelligence, religion, and educational groups, both governments and multinational corporations.

These leaders are the hybrid children and direct descendants of the Orion/Sirian bloodline (the Anunnaki) who created them (and us) millions of years ago. These are their same children who in the past became the future kings and queens, maharajas, generals, political leaders, popes and cardinals and so on. Over thousands and thousands of years of history there have been good guys and bad guys who have guided us through revolutions wars, famines and plagues, to this moment in time where we've all met now in the twenty-first century.

What an exciting time to be alive now, at the beginning of this new era, to wake up from our state of amnesia and be able to understand what is going on around us. We humans are now gradually wakening up to the fact that some of us have been alive for millions of years. We also realise that many of the subjects we studied at school are a pack of lies, and that your granny was once your little boy a few hundred years ago.

But jokes aside, it is blatantly apparent that some parts of the world are in a bad way. War and poverty in parts of Africa and the Middle East, for example, and the unrest amongst the communist nations, whilst there are those, especially the pharmaceutical organisations, arms dealers and banking conglomerates, who are earning obscene amounts of money.

I don't know what the answer is. All I know is that through our DNA many of us are waking up and will be doing so during this new age, and through this global awakening, the future generations will know that there is much to be done to rectify this situation.

To Sum Up

When I was first told that I was expected to write a sequel to *Aquarius* about the UFO and ET phenomenon, I could not for the life of me understand what this had to do with my message in *Aquarius,* which was to explain the soul's journey through the various ages and how the different layers of 'heaven' were structured. My confusion grew as some of the sites I was guided to visit made me feel physically ill. Especially when I read about the dark hidden rituals some of the leaders of our society were participating in. But as time went on and my journey took me from site to site, it gradually dawned on me and became abundantly clear that this was all in *The Great Plan*: everything is as it should be! This had been allowed to happen and the time has come for this festering boil to be lanced.

It is time for a planetary awakening. When we were first created, our DNA was encoded with messages by our creators from the stars, and our DNA molecules were programmed so that when we reached a certain level of intelligence, we would be able to access their information that would 'teach' us about ourselves and how to progress.

The extraterrestrials are here, living among us. Many are our ancestors who have been born into human bodies, also acting as messengers or teachers. Others are from outer space who have materialised into bodies acceptable to dwell amongst us undetected. There are also highly evolved beings living as ordinary humans who receive channelled messages from the Pleiadians, Andromedans and Arcturians. And there are those who live in secret underground bases or hovering in spaceships above us, observing the situation on Earth, especially keeping an eye on the black ops some of the dominant world nations are involved in. Many thousands of years ago, they had left landmarks placed carefully in different parts of the planet for us to discover at a specific time. The most predominant clue, as we've discussed, is the Great Pyramid built on the Giza plateau at the geographical centre of Earth, and aligned to true north and with the constellation Orion. Orion is one of the most prominent and a recognisable constellation in the sky, as its location on the celestial equator allows it to be seen *all over the planet*. It was of great importance to many ancient cultures, and it is no coincidence that the Xi'an Pyramid in China and the Teothihuacan Pyramid in Mexico and the Great Pyramid at Giza Egypt are *all aligned to Orion*.

Then there are the Cambodian temples and their correlation with the constellation Draco – and if you follow the procession of Earth (and the slow wobble of Earth over thousands of years around the North Star) it is noticed that the Sphinx points right to the constellation Leo on the spring equinox of every year, and has done since 10,500 BC

In the Great Pyramid, in the king's chamber, the air shafts point to Orion and Draco. In the queen's chamber, the air shafts point to Sirius and Ursa Minor. The constellation of Ursa Minor was only introduced in 600 BC, but the ancient Egyptians considered Ursa Major and Minor to be part of Draco (known to the ancient Egyptians as the Hippo). Draco was associated with the goddess Tawret (who took the form of a hippo.)

It is quite obvious, in summary, that all the clues harp back to 10,500, which takes us to the biblical flood of Noah, and other well-documented accounts of a catastrophic world deluge. The gods, who after all created us in their image, are people who look like us; the only difference is that they are thousands of years more advanced than us. But they got rather carried away, and had made such a mess of their creations that the founders decided to create a flood, and whether real or organised, is neither here nor there – the flood happened. What was left of the world's civilizations virtually had to start from scratch again, with the guidance once again of those who created us. It is from this point that the myth of each nation's creation starts from. Be it from serpents coming up from the ground, or beings coming from the skies, it is from then the nations of the planet gradually grew into who we are now . . . just as we have to learn about the ETs now.

In closing I am quoting from Pat Lee's *Extraterrestrial Compendium*:

'Humans comprise many sub-races and cultures of people. They communicate through different spoken languages and have under-developed telepathic capabilities. Humans on Earth are a very young race with rudimentary technology, still largely mechanical and powered by the combustion of fossil fuels. Only recently have concerted efforts been made to look at alternative, sustainable technologies. Humans are also probably the only race in the galaxy using a monetary system, something other intelligent extraterrestrials have long since abandoned. Mostly unaware of anything beyond their immediate world, humans routinely kill each other to satisfy emotional, political and physical needs.'

Final Thoughts

I am just a messenger who had been instructed to gather this information together into a book as a sequel to *The Dawn of the Age of Aquarius.*

I hope you enjoy this further insight into Earth's mysteries, its gods, and growing awareness that we do indeed have ancestors from the stars, and enjoy browsing through the suggested websites and YouTube presentations below.

June Rye
August 2017

oooOooo

Suggested Sites to Visit

http://wespenre.com/
http://wespenre.com/human-origins-and-the-living-library.htm
https://www.bibliotecapleyades.net/esp_historia_humanidad.htm
http://www.exopoliticshongkong.com/
https://www.bibliotecapleyades.net/vida_alien/esp_vida_alien_19a.htm
https://www.bibliotecapleyades.net/esp_autor_lyssaroyal.htm
http://www.exopaedia.org/Exopolitics
https://www.bibliotecapleyades.net/sociopolitica/master_file/masterfile.htm

Popular Videos

Timothy Good: NEED TO KNOW: UFOs, THE MILITARY, AND INTELLIGENCE – MUFON SYMPOSIUM
https://www.youtube.com/watch?v=jre3BNlBFF4

Michael Tellinger: Vanished Gold-Mining Civilization of South Africa FULL LECTURE Part 1
https://www.youtube.com/watch?v=dtjX0qxHkNI

Graham Hancock: Magicians of the Gods - The Great Flood, Atlantis, and Megaliths [2014]
https://www.youtube.com/watch?v=_KZLPS1ELDc

David Hatcher Childress: Stone Balls, Obelisks, Tesla, and the Moon
https://www.youtube.com/watch?v=Rs0I0ZoPLHM

Proof of Ancient Anunnaki Technology Discovered All Over the World [FULL VIDEO]
https://www.youtube.com/watch?v=tKAElhgSFaw

Documentary - ANCIENT MAN-MADE TUNNELS - Underground Civilizations
https://www.youtube.com/watch?v=9_0KTT7UuoE

Documentary on Anunnaki Theory: Were We Genetically Engineered? https://www.youtube.com/watch?v=caX5j5EHbVc

Ancient Pyramids Proof that Recorded History is Wrong [FULL VIDEO]
https://www.youtube.com/watch?v=ga4DuJOqPqM

Klaus Dona: The Hidden History of the Human Race
https://www.youtube.com/watch?v=syWq6_oVhD0

The Anunnaki Series S1E1: Who Are the Anunnaki?
https://www.youtube.com/watch?v=YkQfpYkgO48

UFO Encounters with the World Militaries - Richard Dolan
https://www.youtube.com/watch?v=LIc3Atezq8E

Aliens Are Here, Proof UFOs are Hiding Deep in Our Oceans [FULL VIDEO]
Paul Stonehill
https://www.youtube.com/watch?v=XrqQpwPv6HA

Wayne Herschel: Hidden Records BC - Megalithomania South Africa - FULL LECTURE
https://www.youtube.com/watch?v=Jc9xo_u5FGk

200,000-Year-Old Ancient Levitation Technology That Defies the Laws of Physics
https://www.youtube.com/watch?v=7CzCDR0nv5g

www.ingramcontent.com/pod-product-compliance
Lightning Source LLC
LaVergne TN
LVHW010305070426
835507LV00027B/3444